Bankers Wankers!

MORGANTO

Welcome to Bankers Wankers!

Who loves bankers? We don't!

Enjoy!

Join our mailing list! Also, limited edition prints signed by the artist and downloadable high definition digital images are available through www.Mordanto.com and www.BankersWankers.com

Also by Mordanto:
Cartoon History of the Financial Crisis
Art of the Recession, Vols 1 & 2

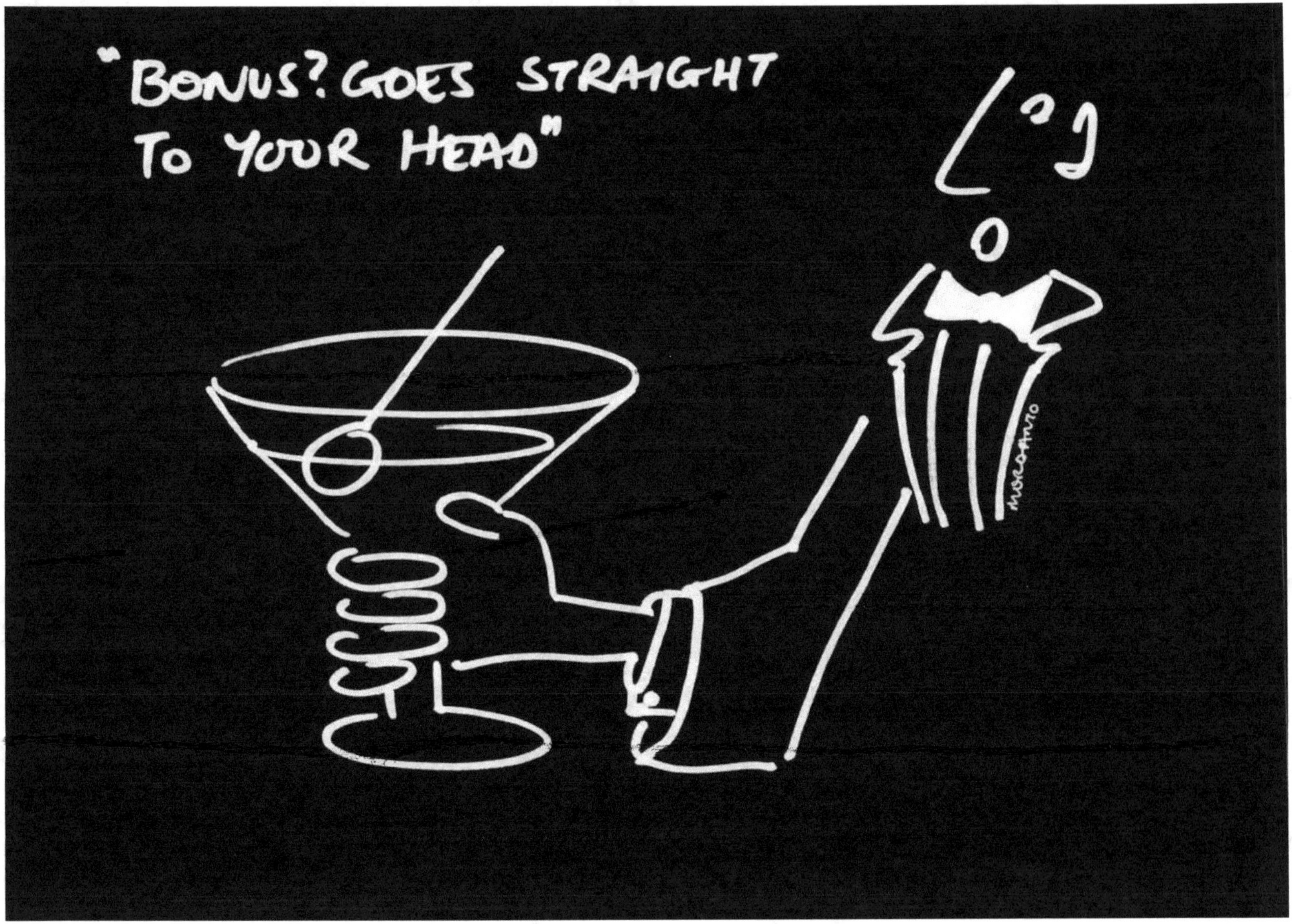
"BONUS?. GOES STRAIGHT TO YOUR HEAD"

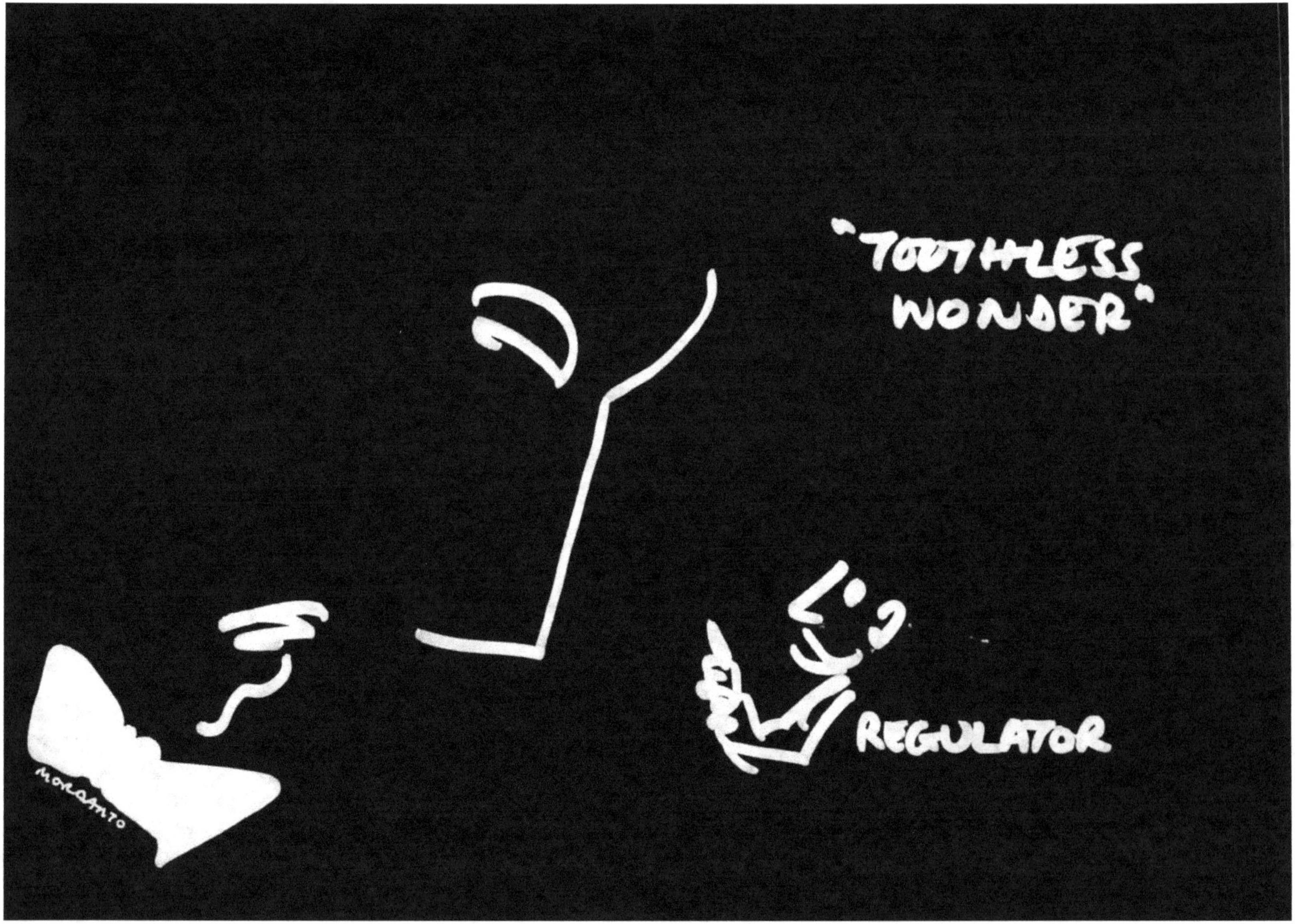
"TOOTHLESS WONDER"
REGULATOR
MORGANTO

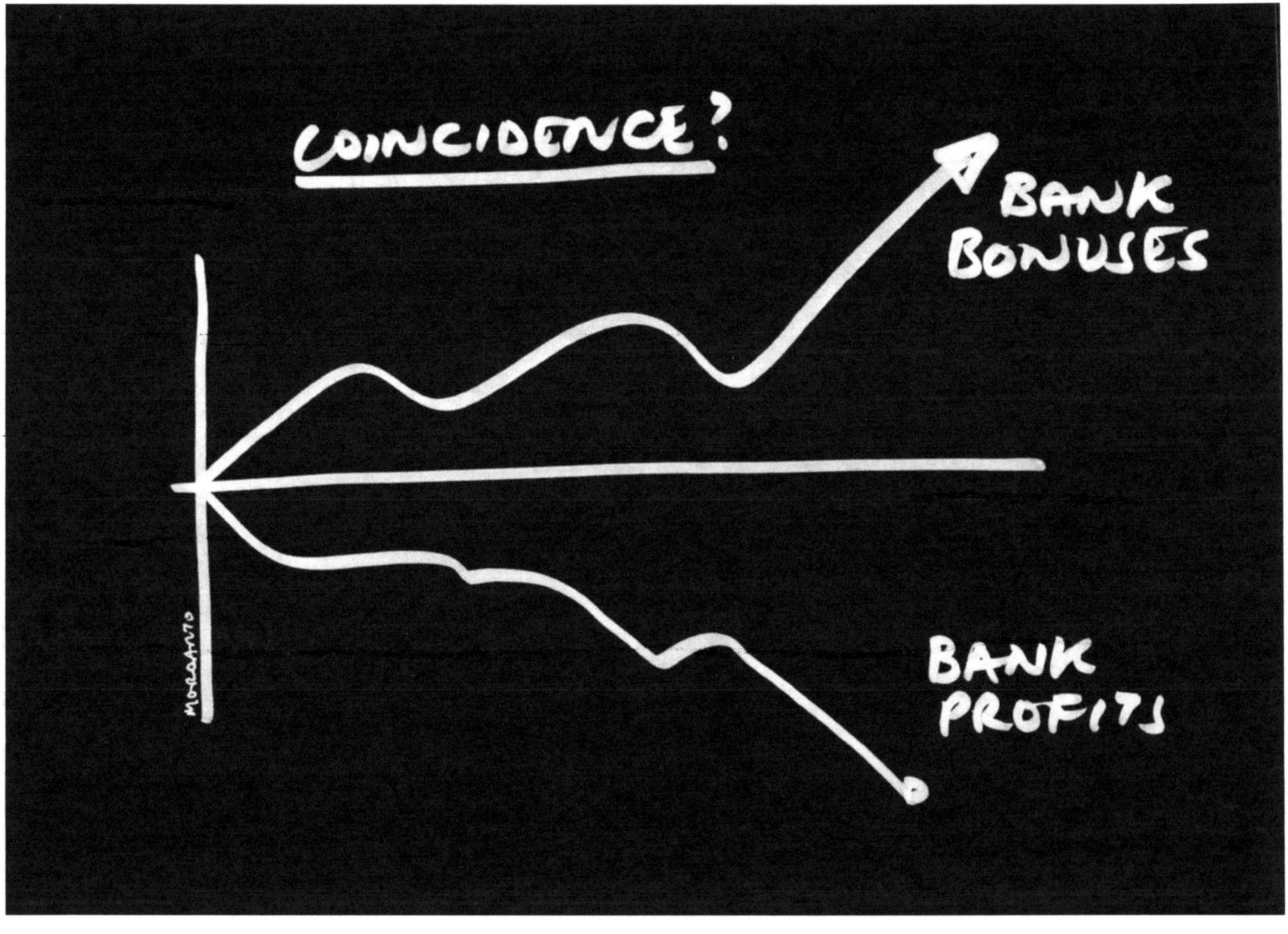
COINCIDENCE?
BANK BONUSES
BANK PROFITS

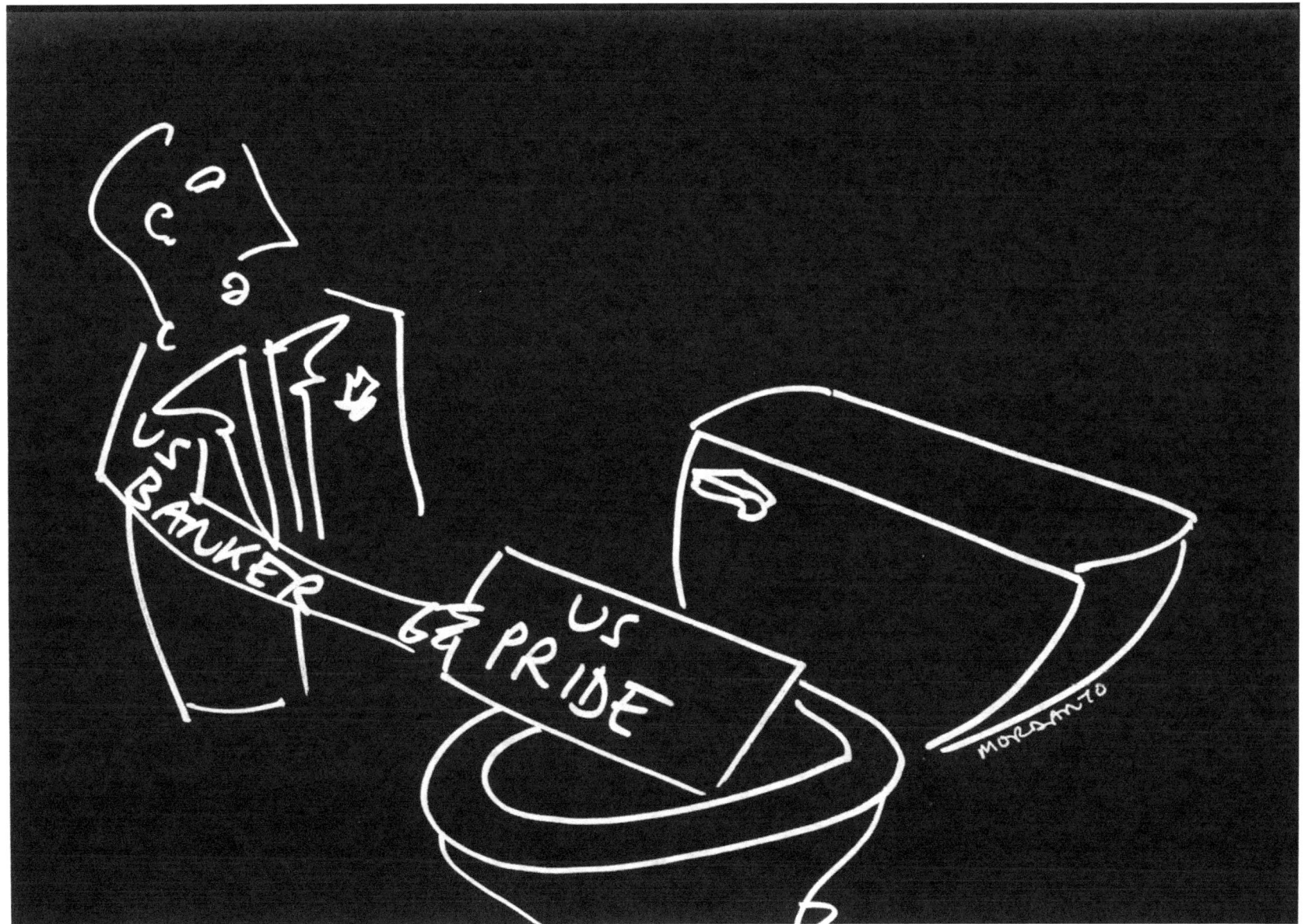

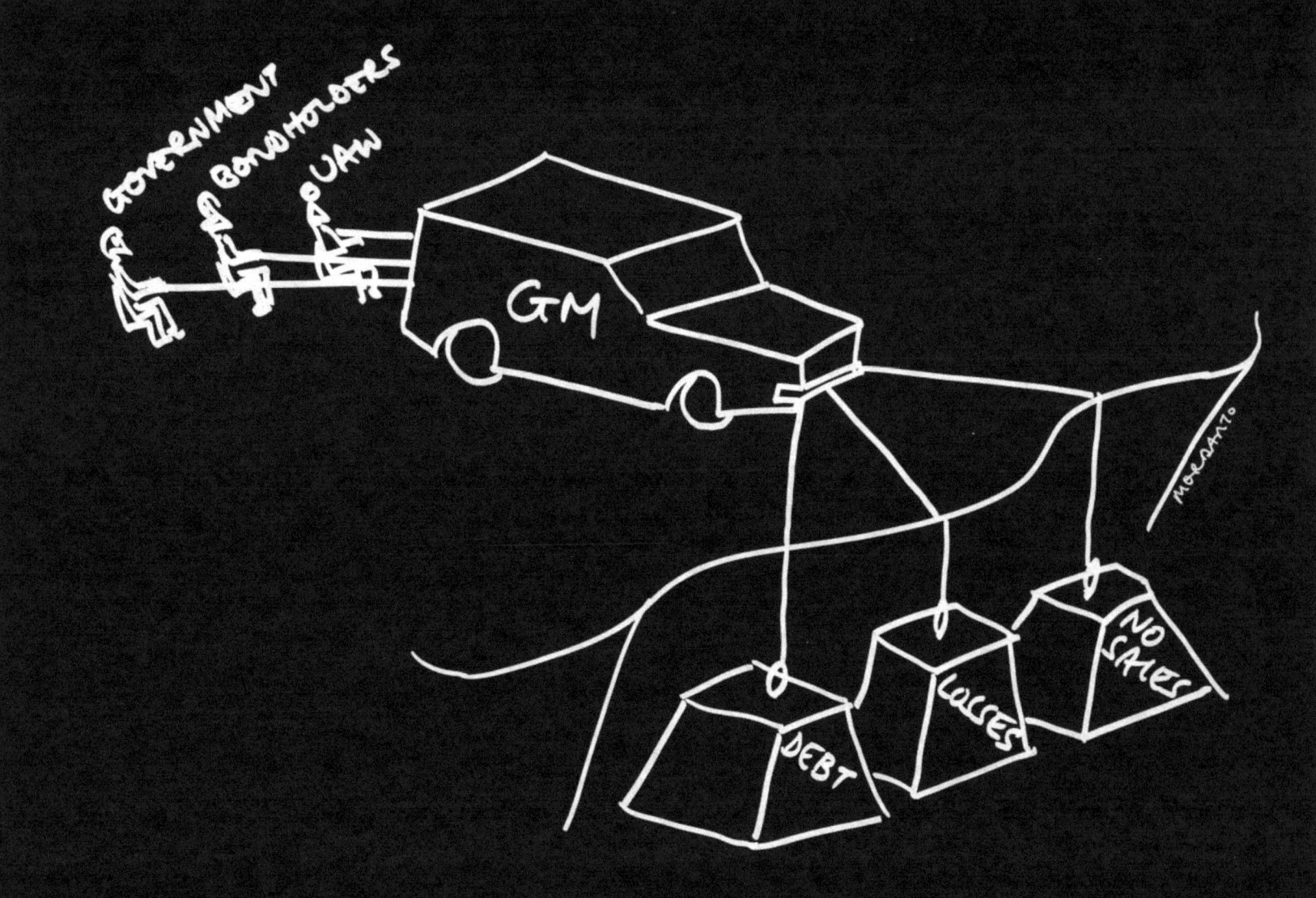

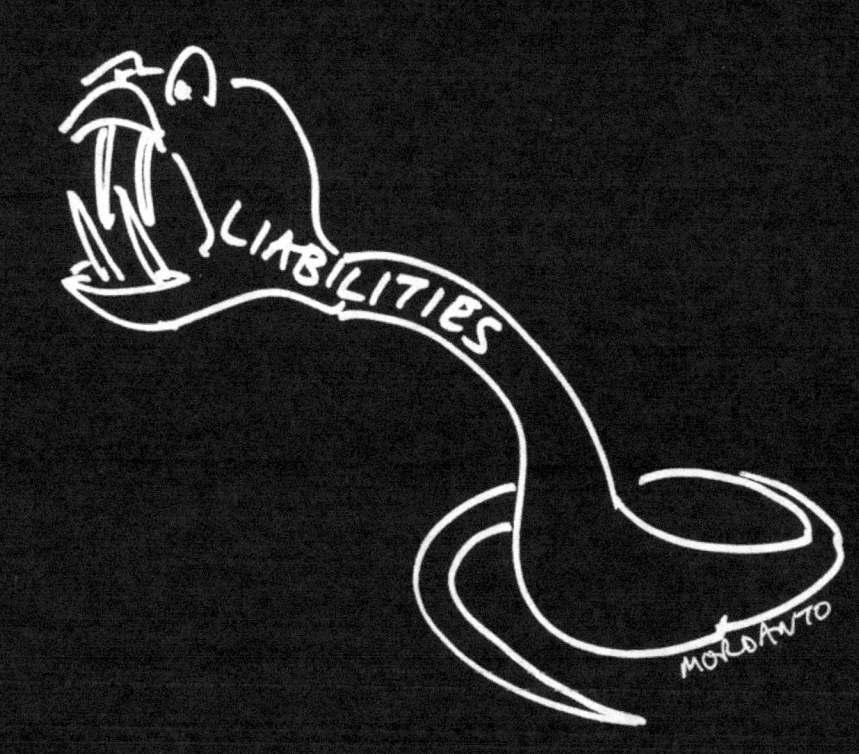

"NOT MY CHOSEN PROFESSION"

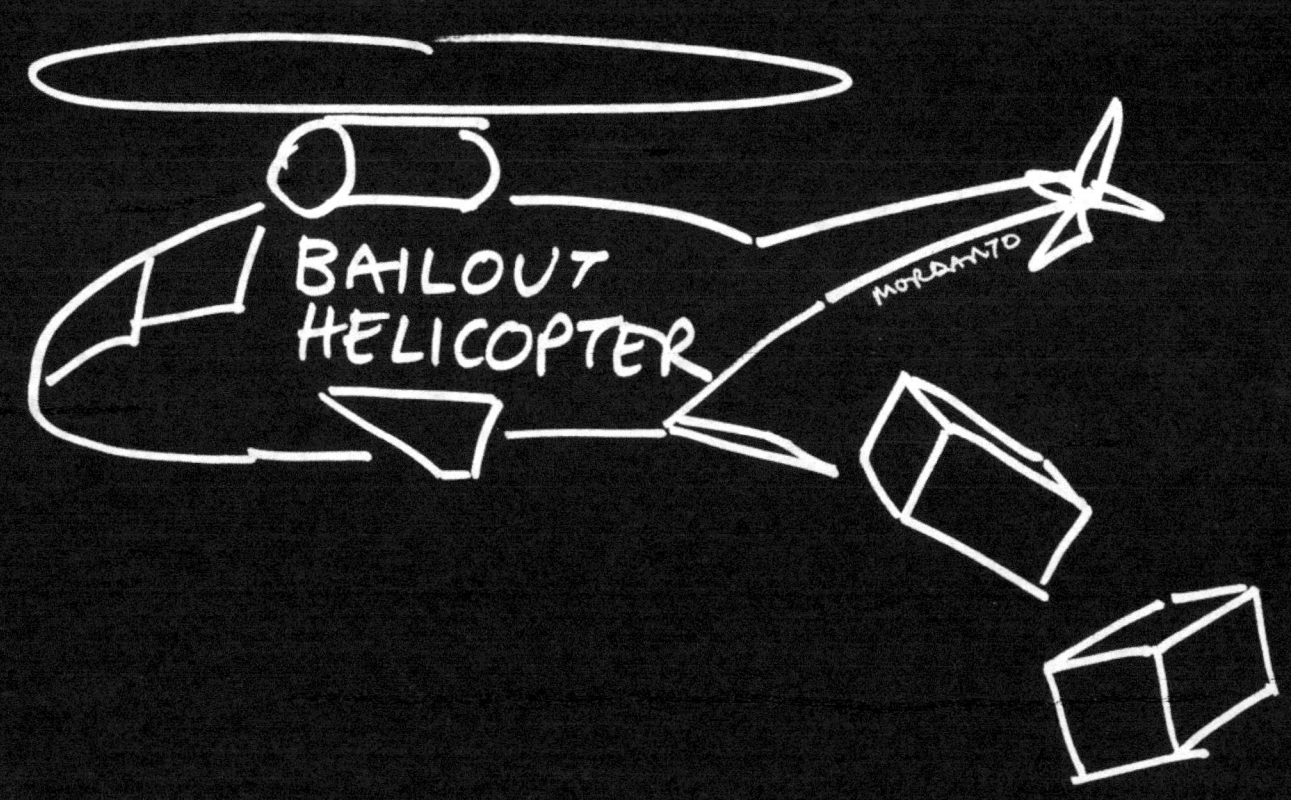

5=

AVERAGE NUMBER OF
EXPENSIVE WATCHES OWNED
BY LEHMAN TRADERS

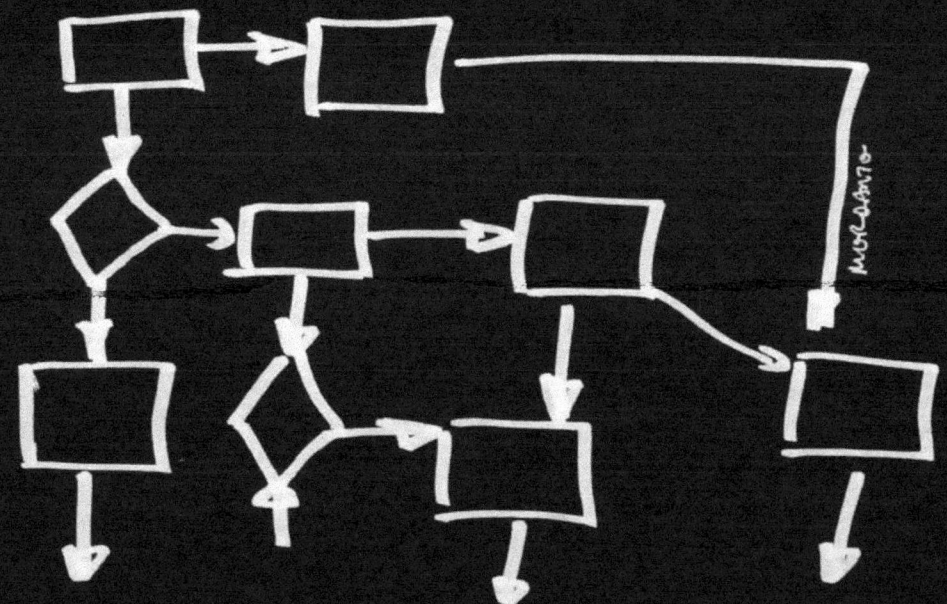

"US TAX CODE"

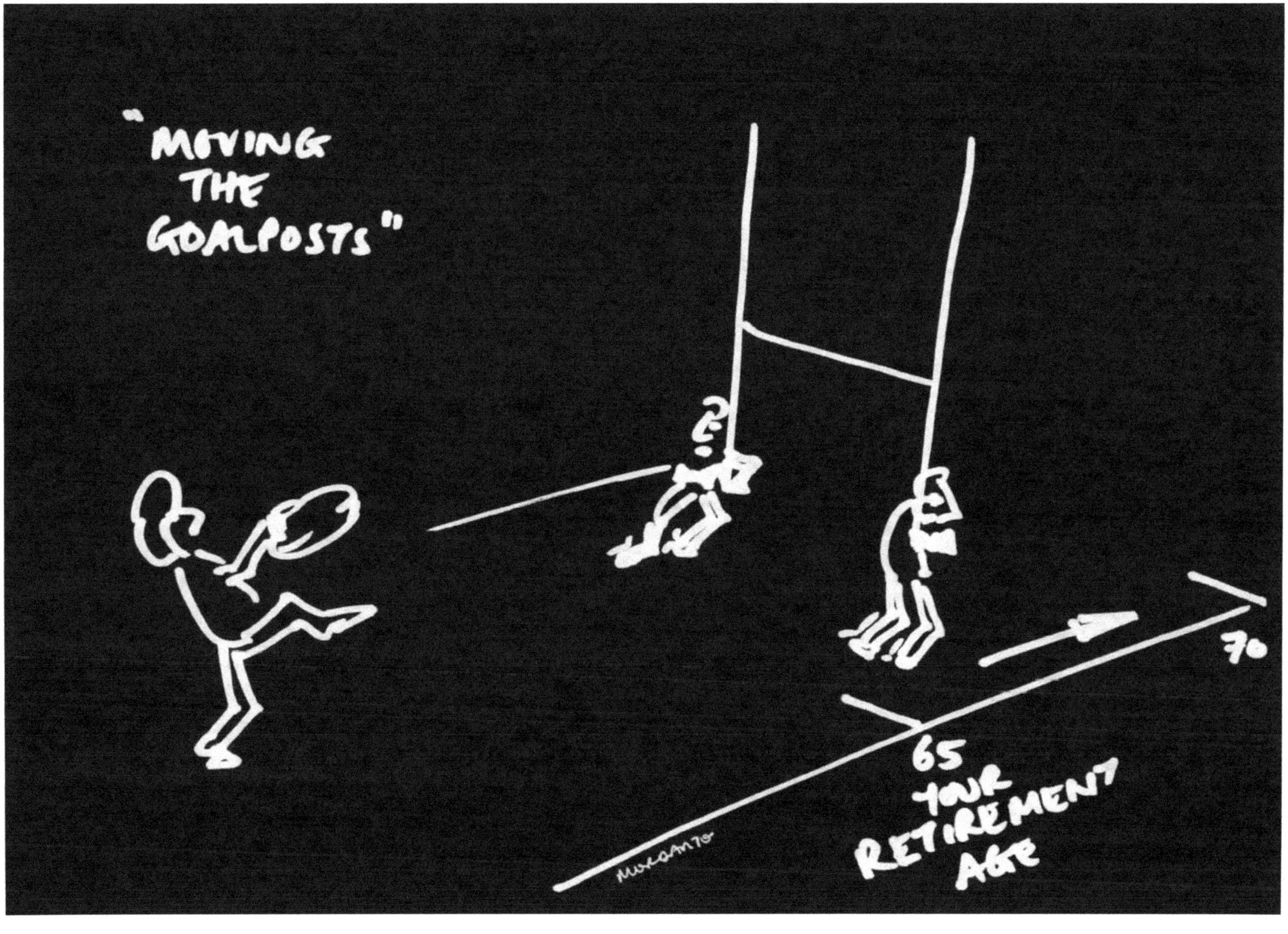
"MOVING THE GOALPOSTS"
70
65
YOUR RETIREMENT AGE

"IT'S NOT A LAYOFF...
YOU ARE NOT BEING FIRED.
YOU ARE BEING OFFERED
INDEFINITE, UNPAID LEAVE."

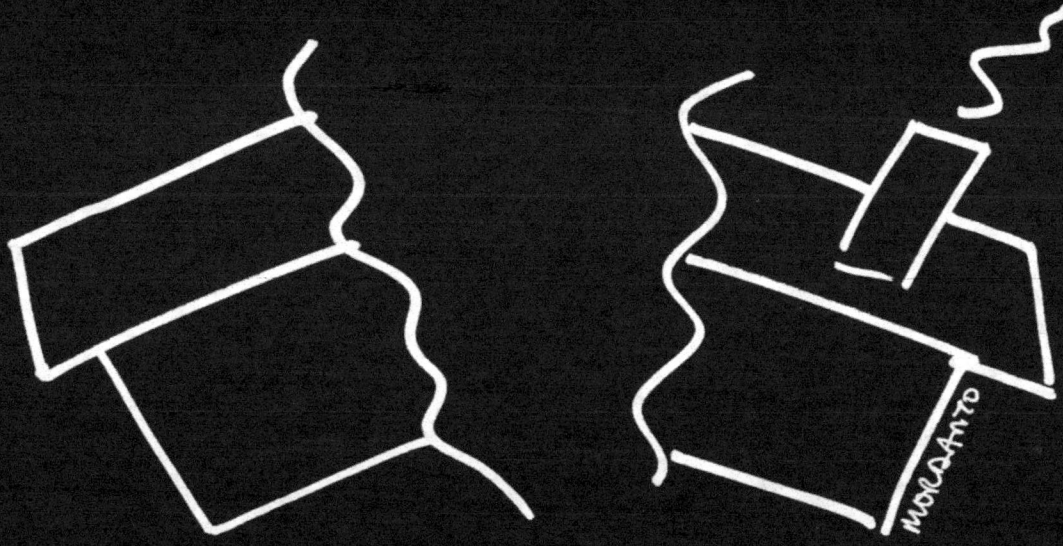

"BROKEN DREAMS"

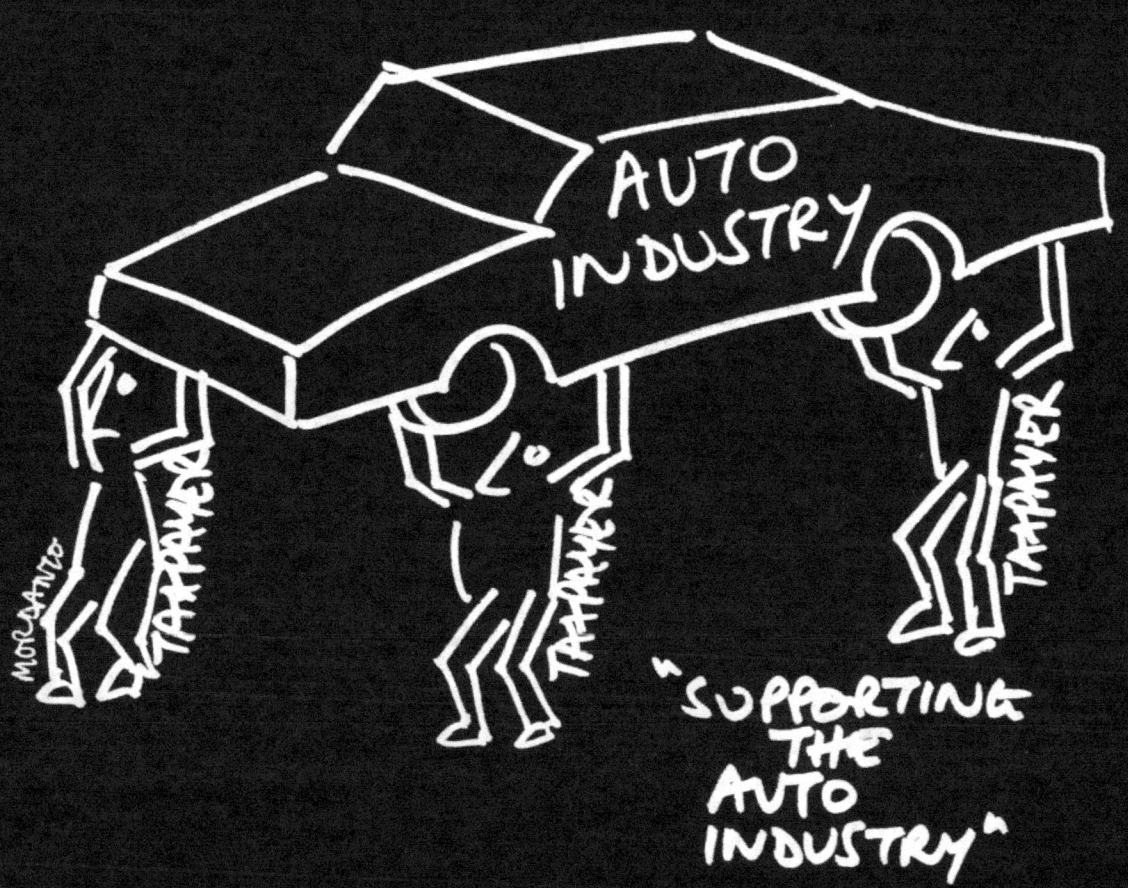

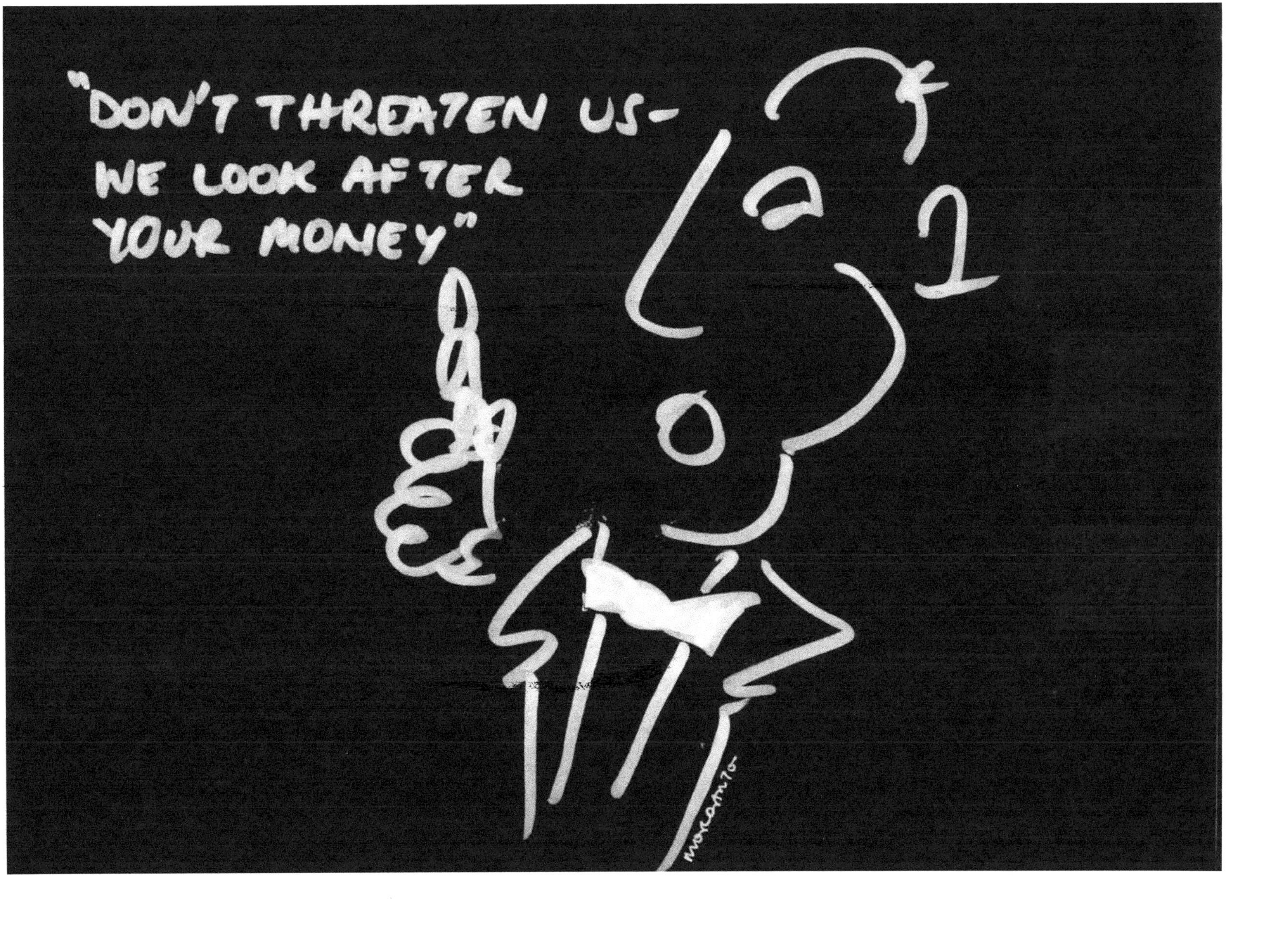
"DON'T THREATEN US-
WE LOOK AFTER
YOUR MONEY"

"BANKING'S FINEST"

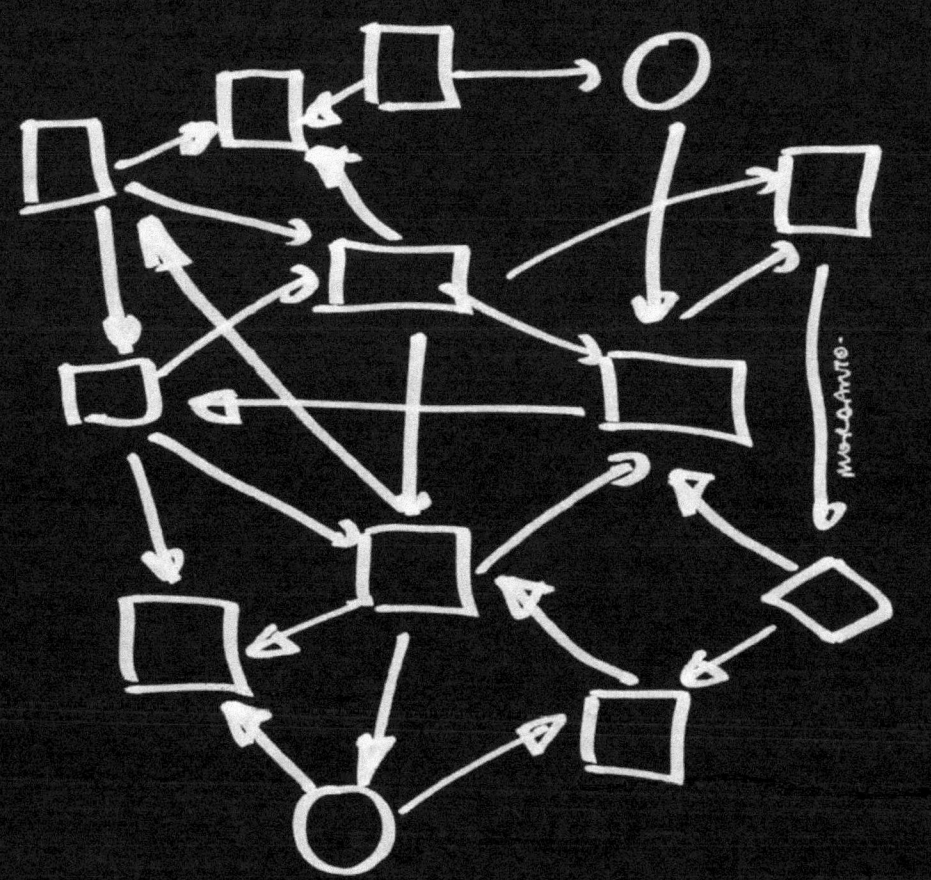

"THE
SYSTEM
MUST
BE
SAVED"

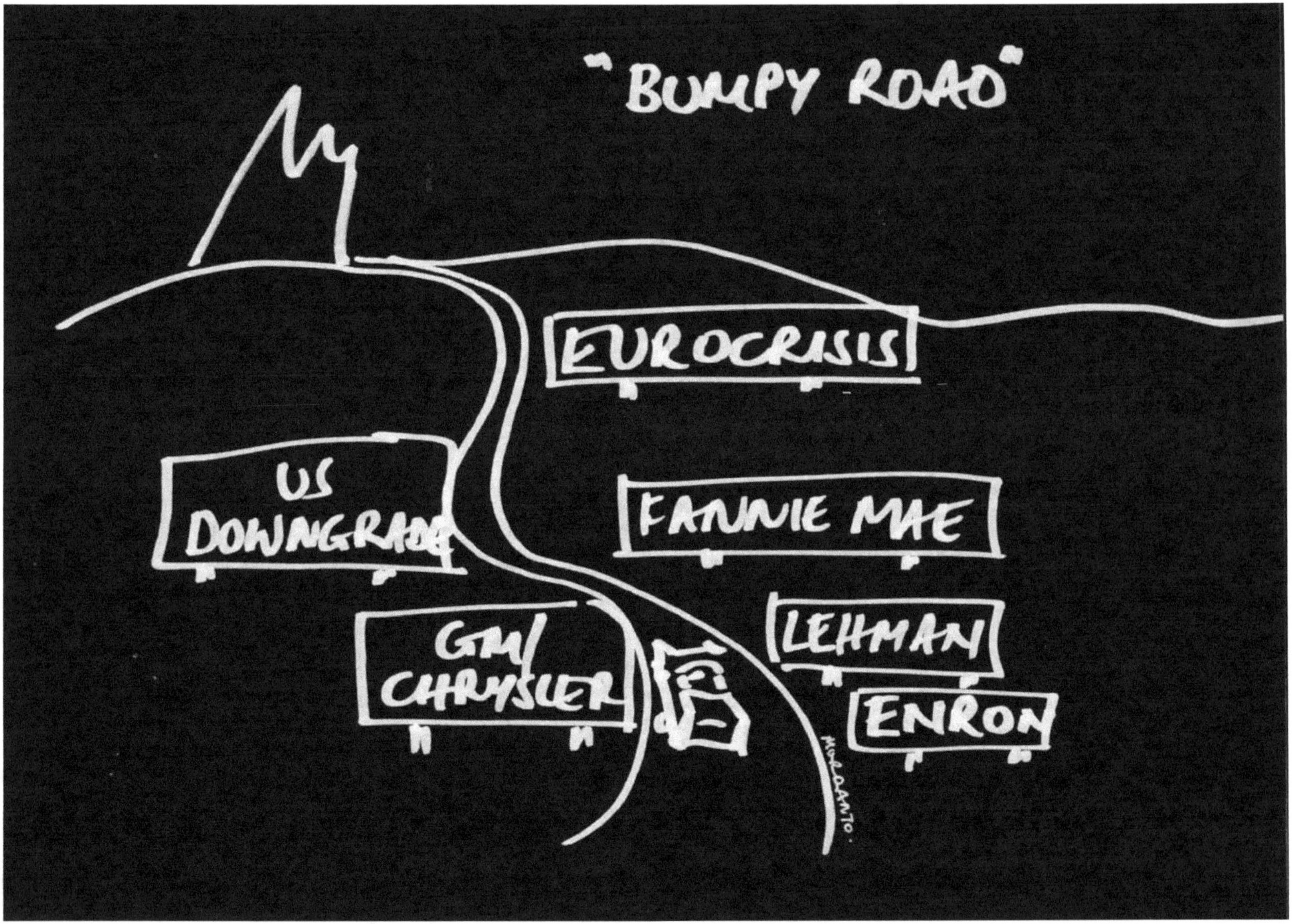
"BUMPY ROAD"
EUROCRISIS
US DOWNGRADE
FANNIE MAE
GM/ CHRYSLER
LEHMAN
ENRON

"OIL PRICE VOLATILITY"

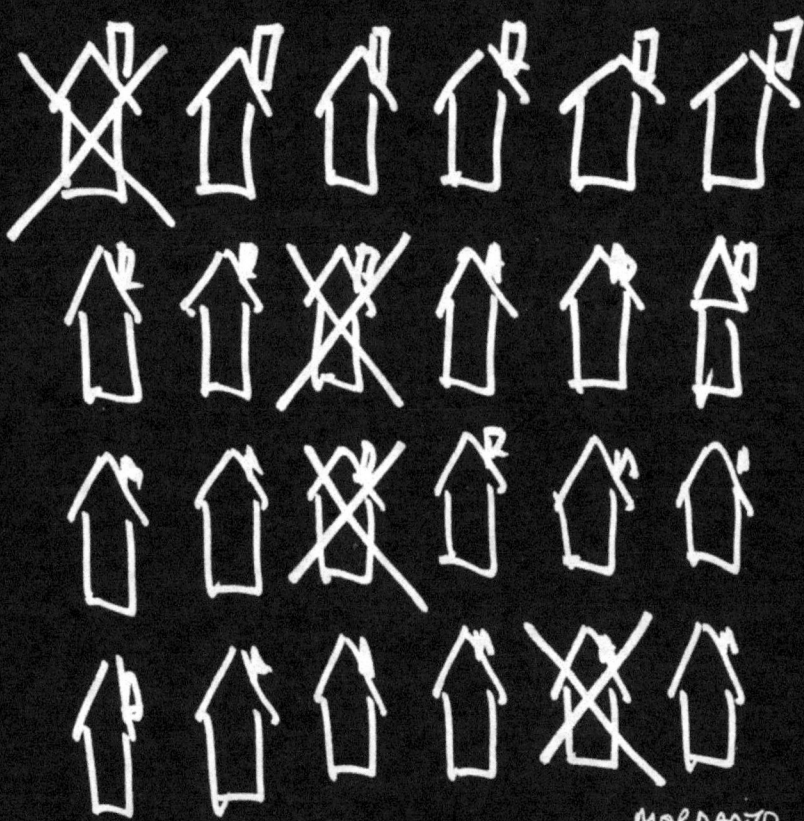

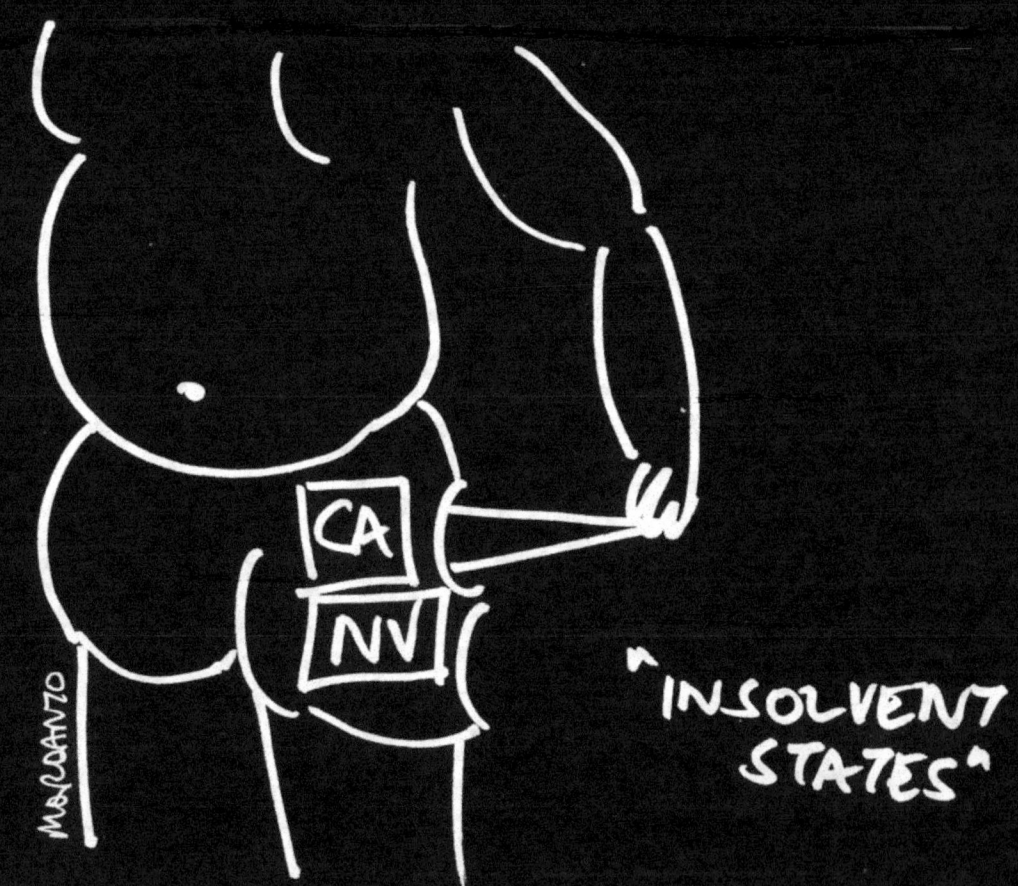

"UNDER
WATER"

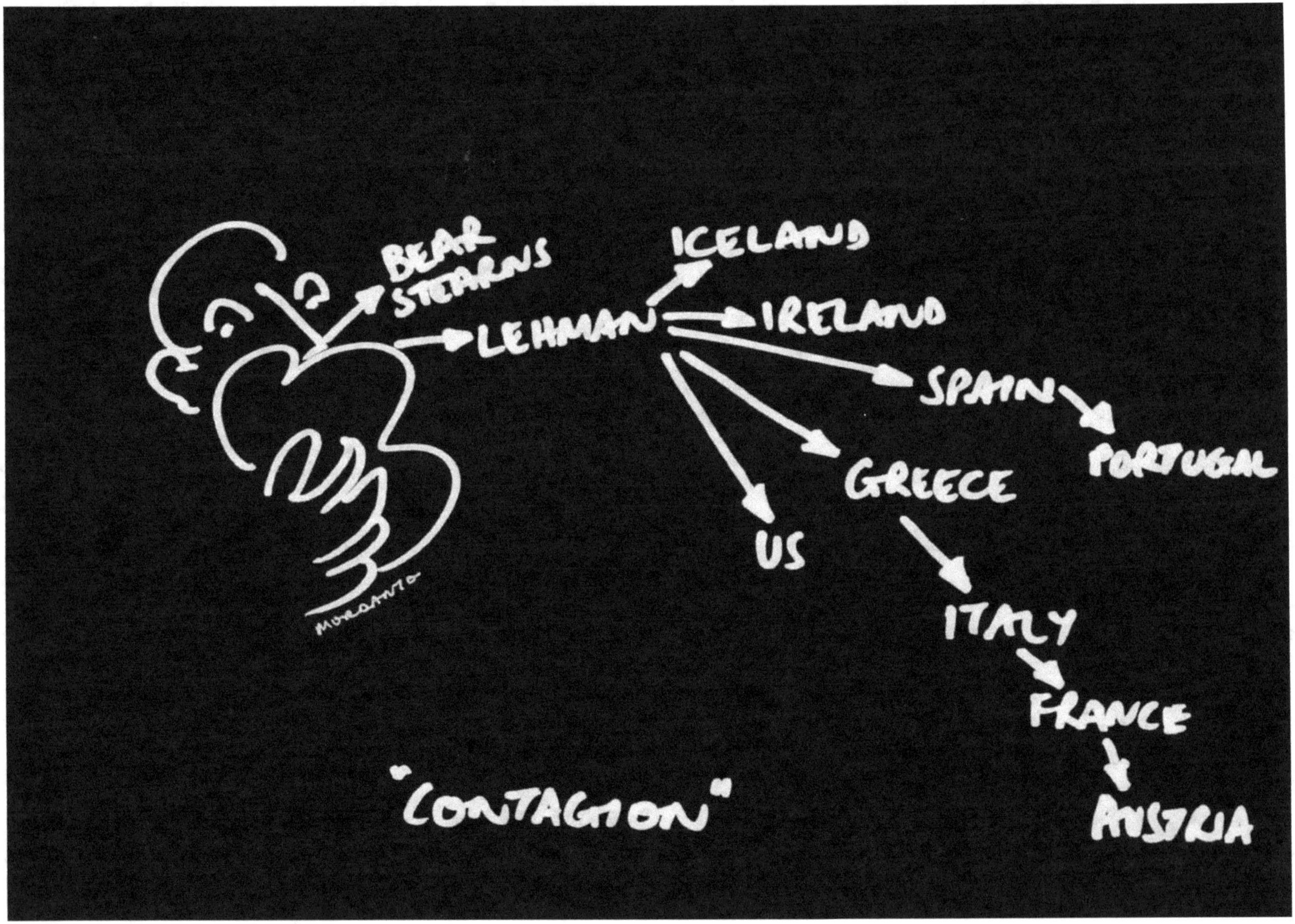

BEAR STEARNS

ICELAND

LEHMAN

IRELAND

SPAIN

PORTUGAL

US

GREECE

ITALY

FRANCE

AUSTRIA

"CONTAGION"

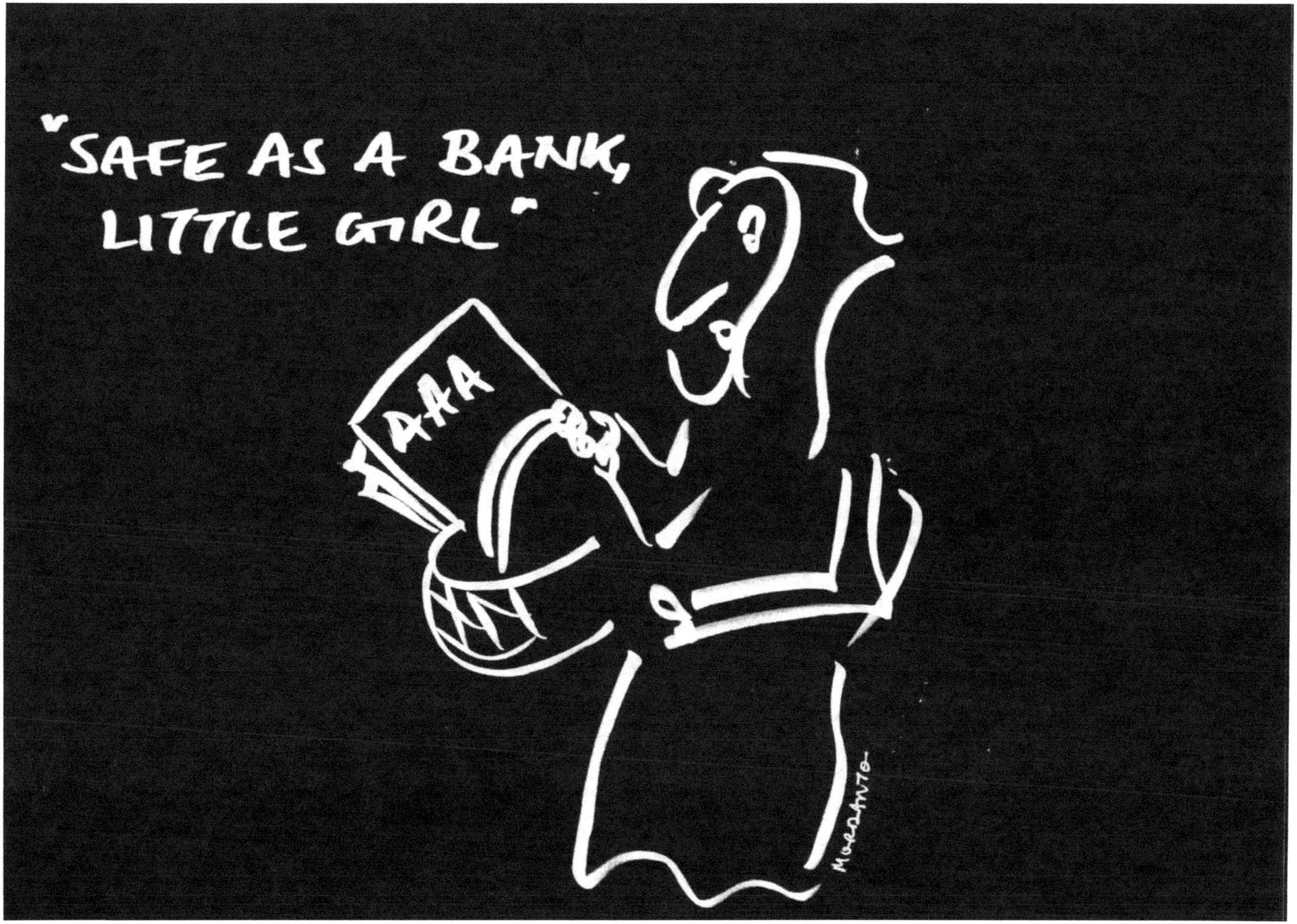
"SAFE AS A BANK,
LITTLE GIRL"
AAA
MORDANTO

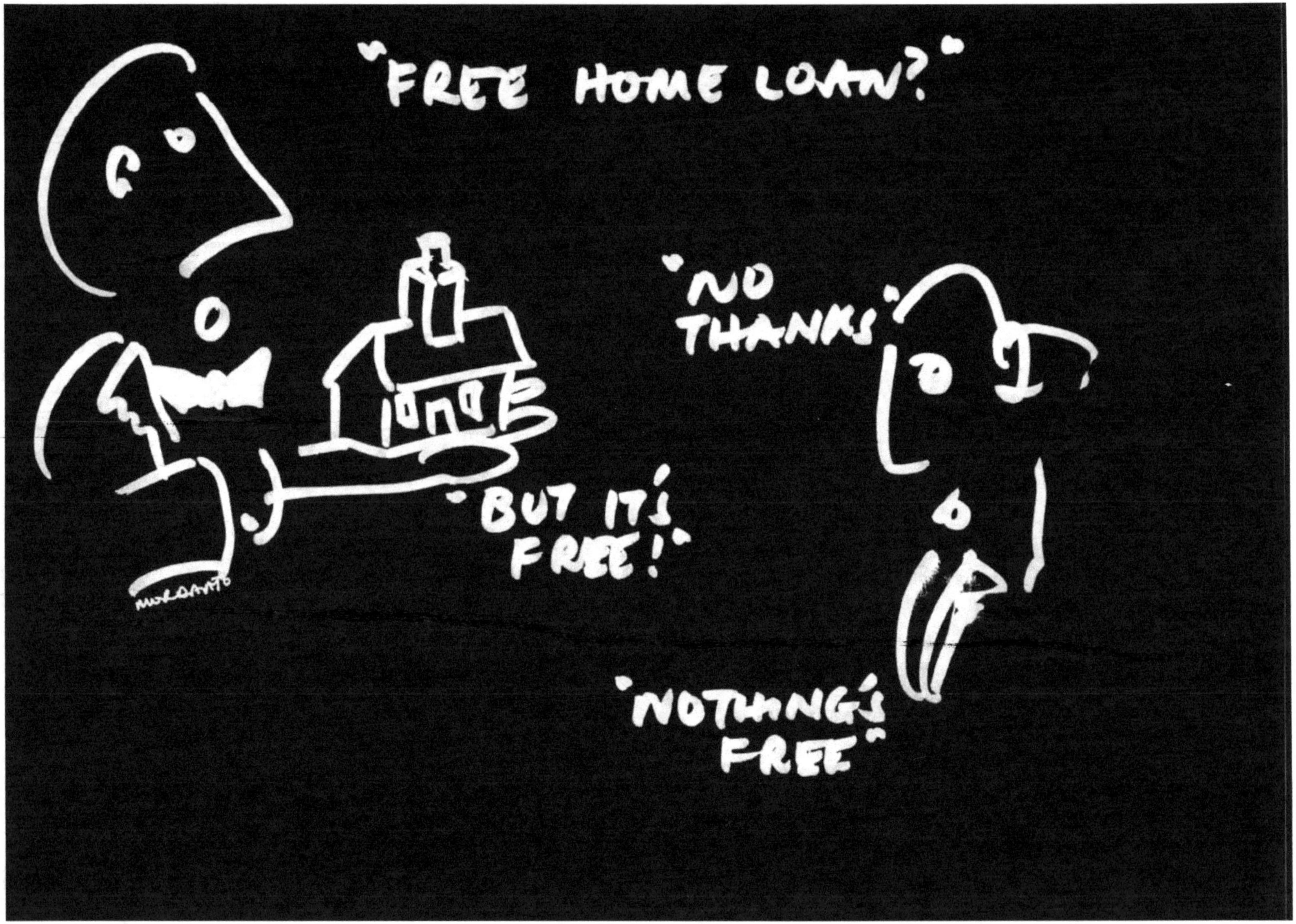

"FREE HOME LOAN?"
"NO THANKS"
"BUT IT'S FREE!"
"NOTHING'S FREE"

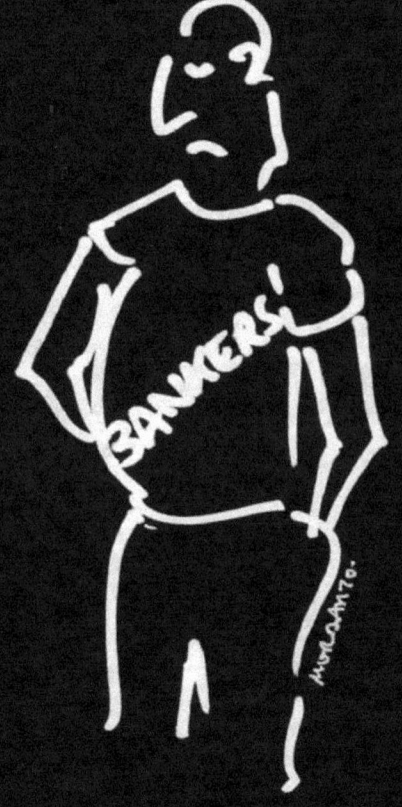

"BANKERS LOOTED ME & ALL I GOT WAS THIS LOUSY T-SHIRT"

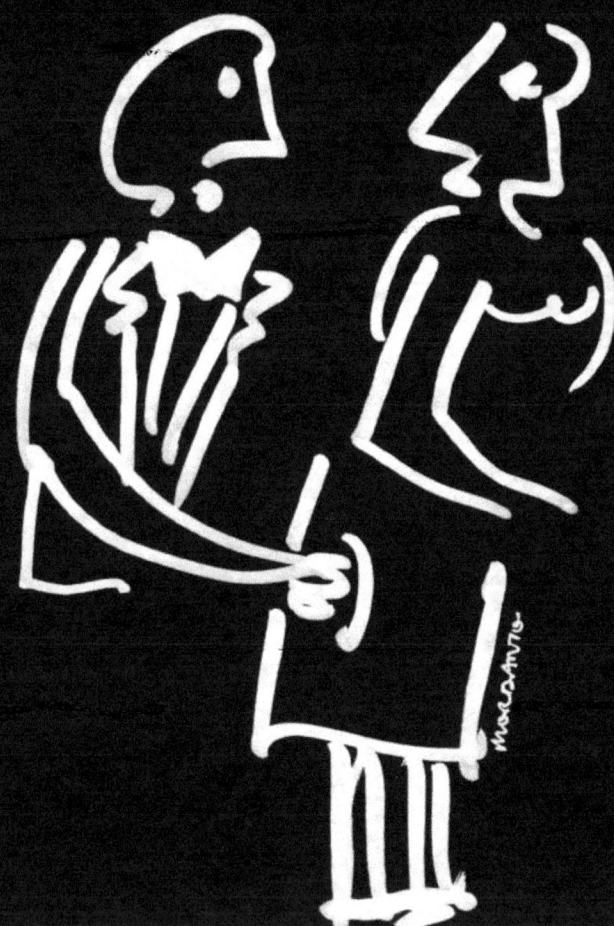

"LONG-RANGE
ECONOMIC
FORECASTING"

"DROWNING IN DEBT"

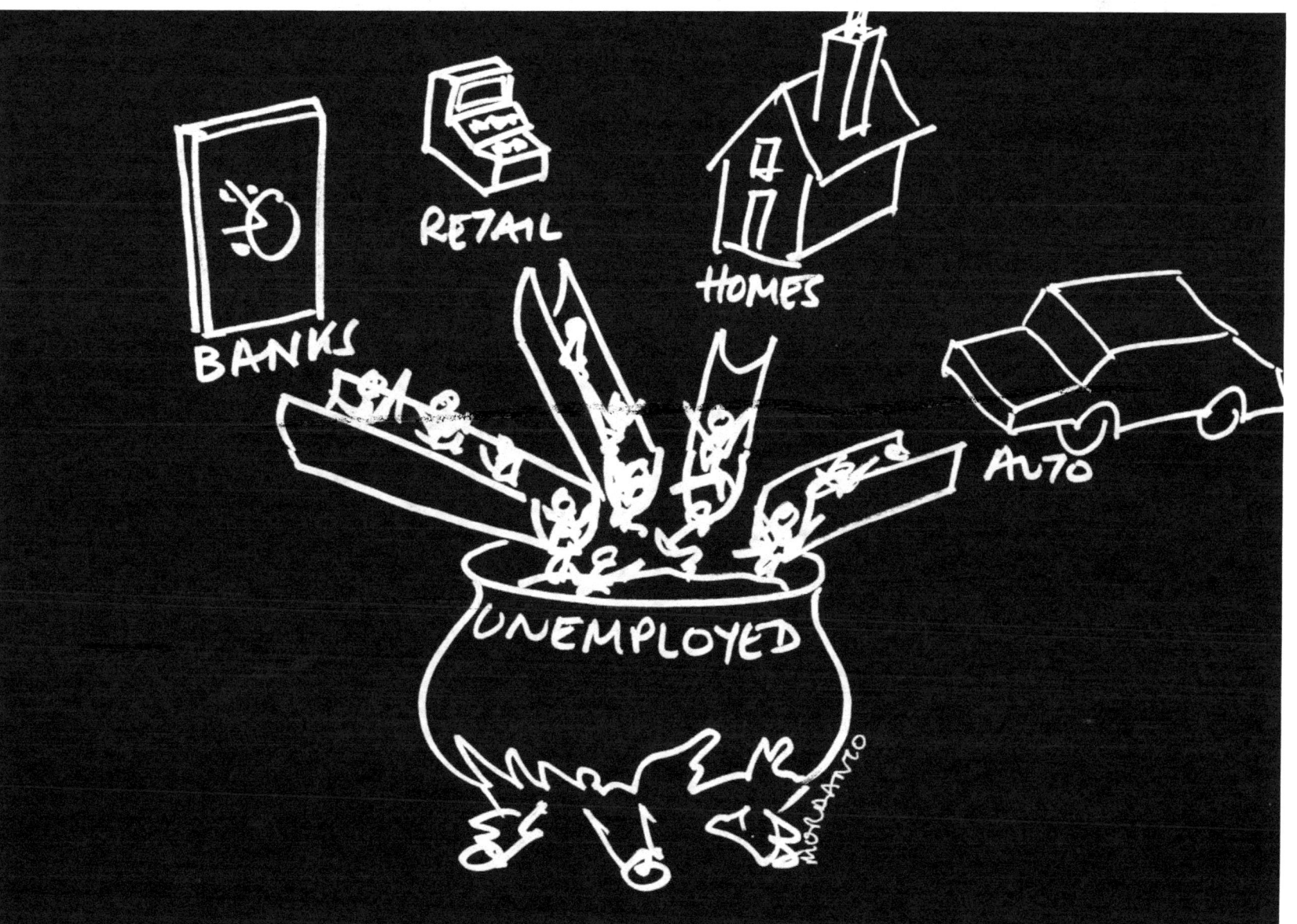

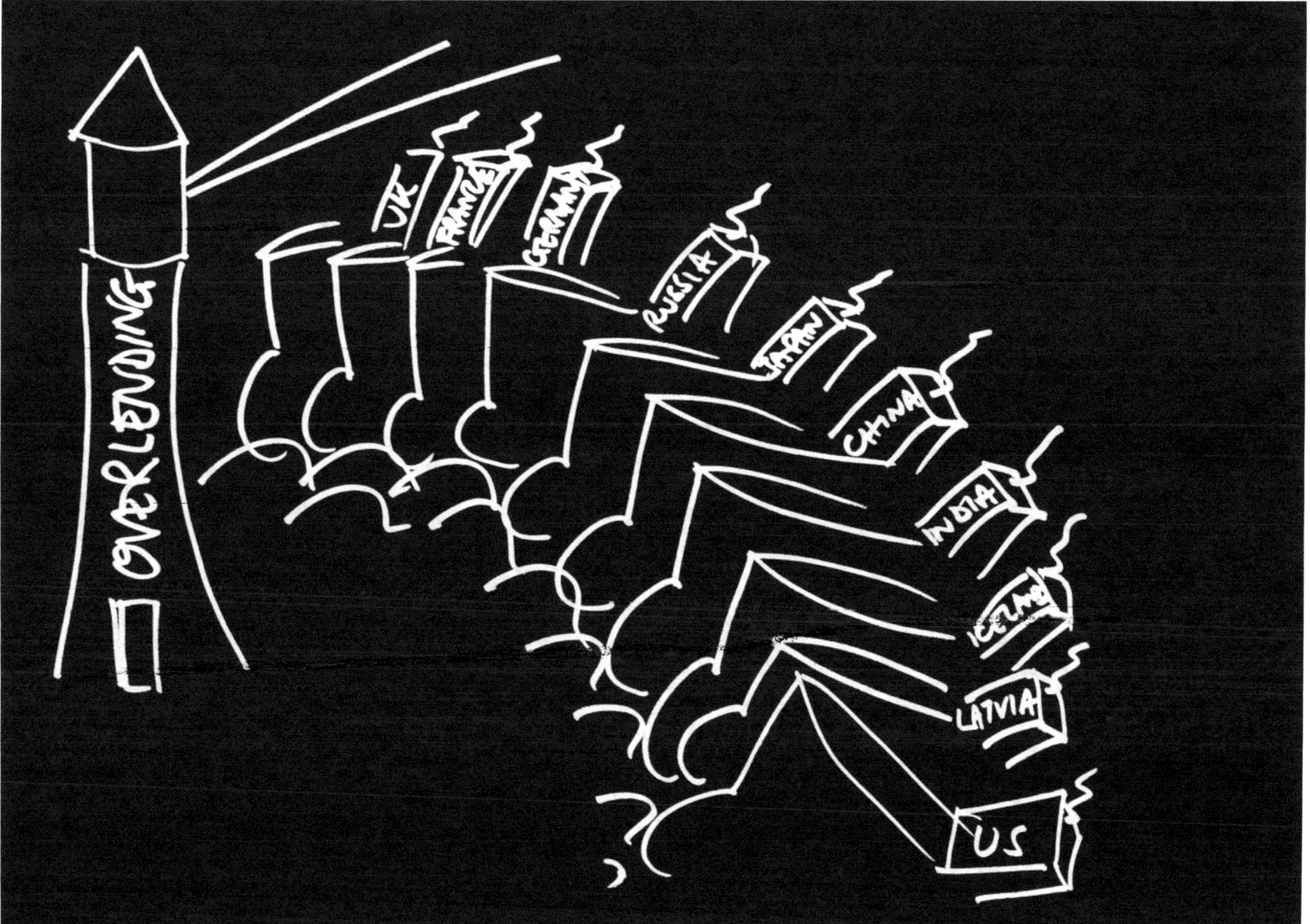

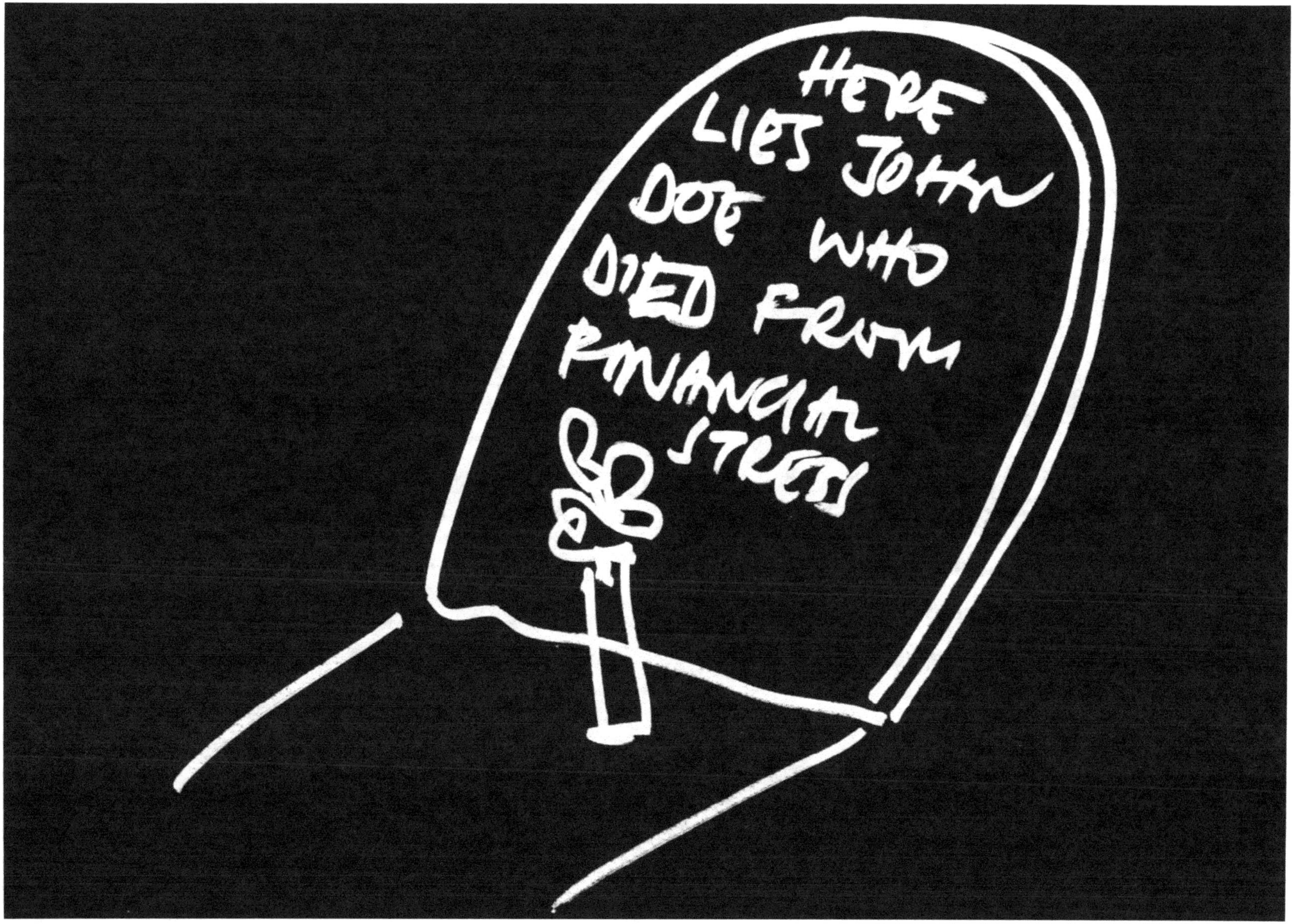
HERE
LIES JOHN
DOE WHO
DIED FROM
FINANCIAL
STRESS

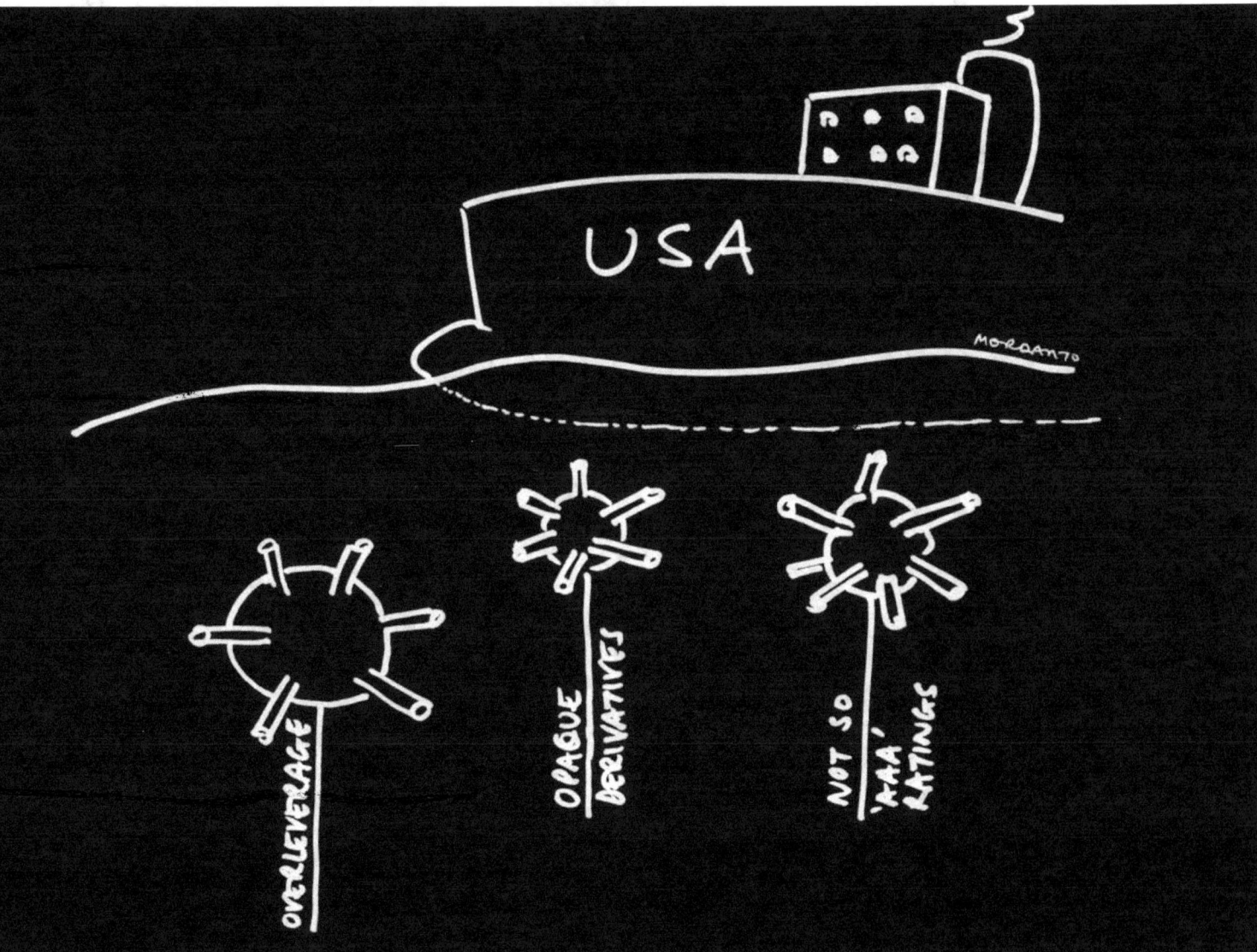

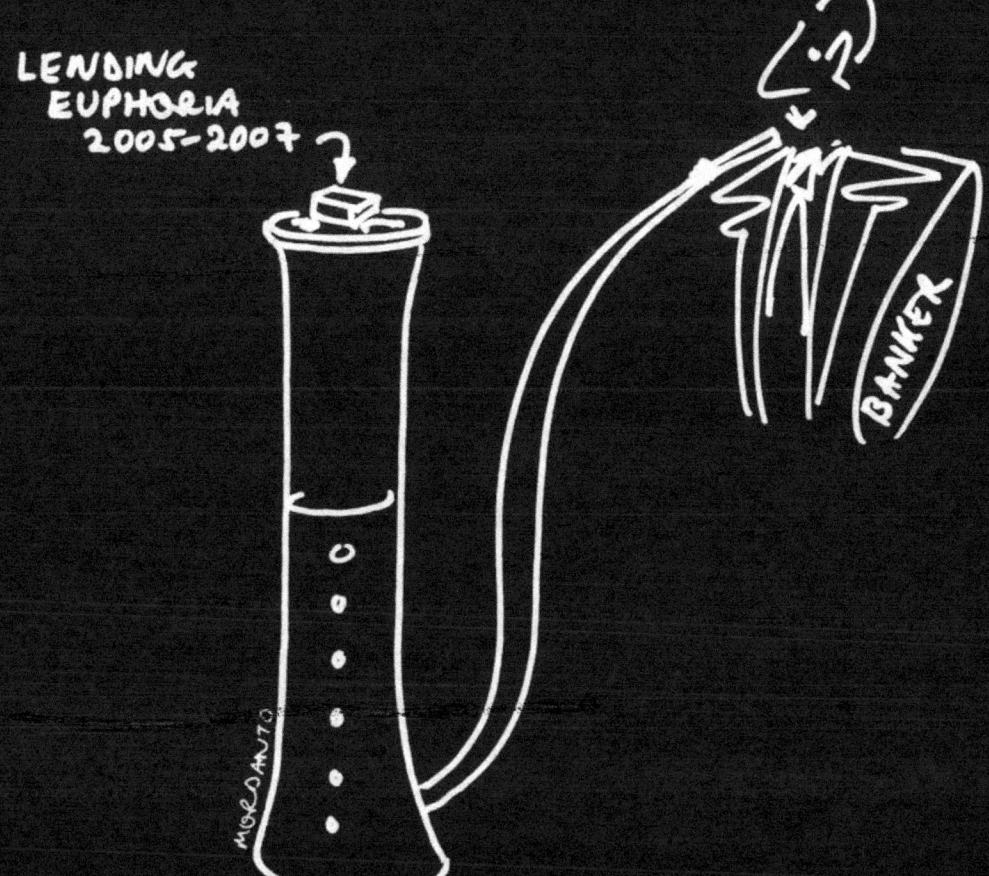

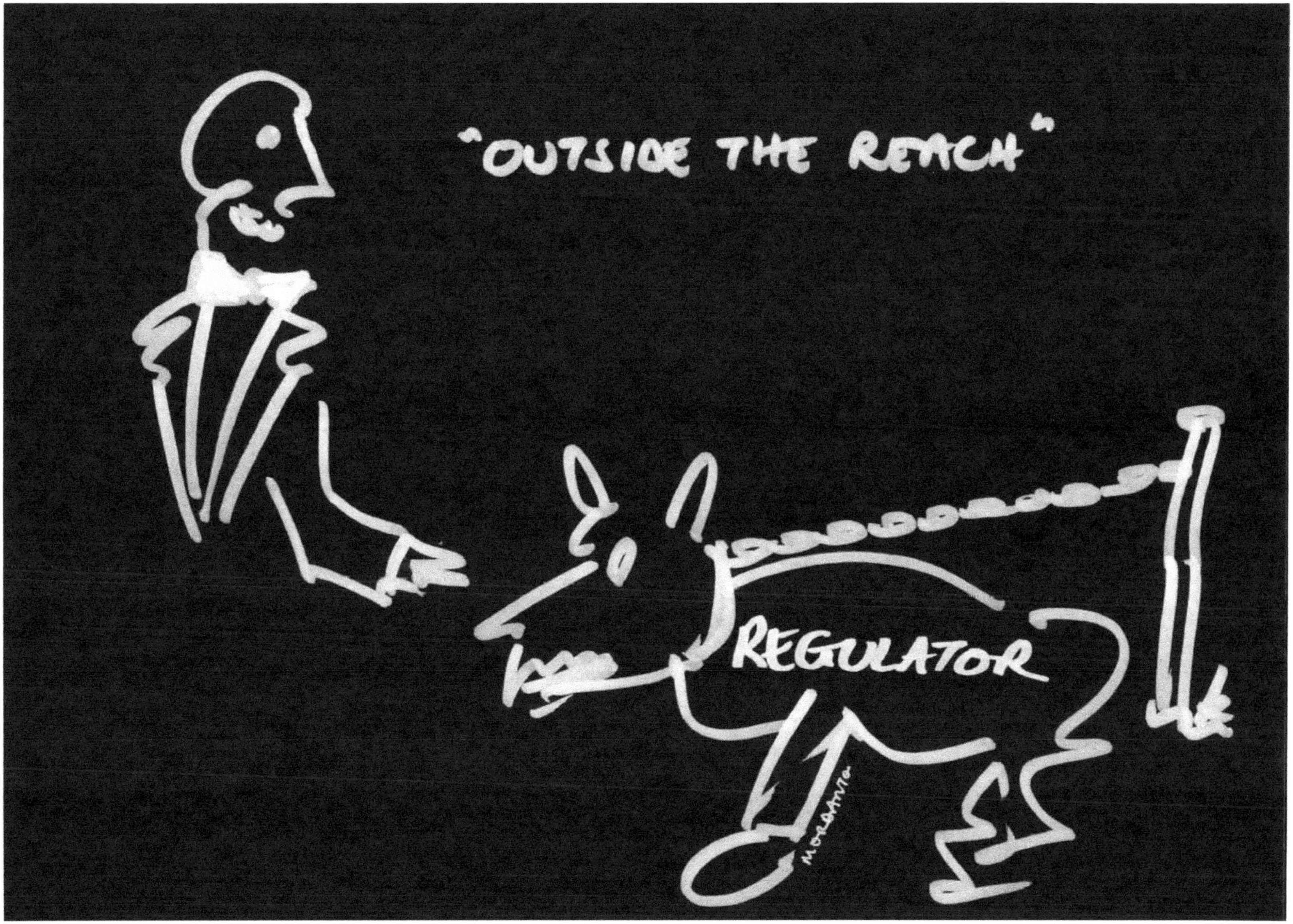
"OUTSIDE THE REACH"
REGULATOR

"UGLY SISTERS AT THE BALL"

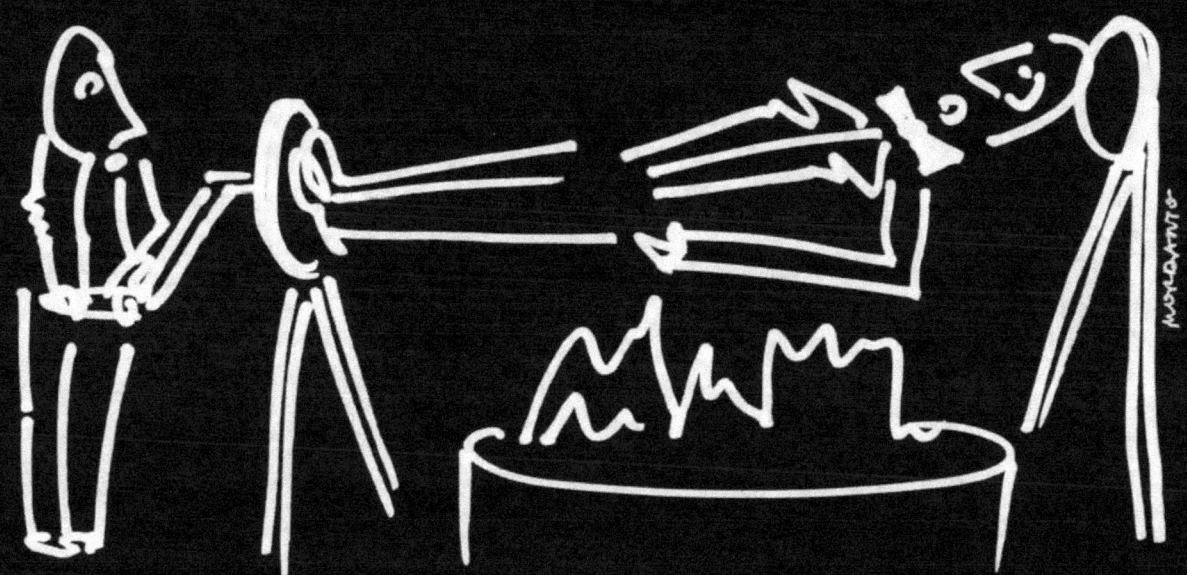

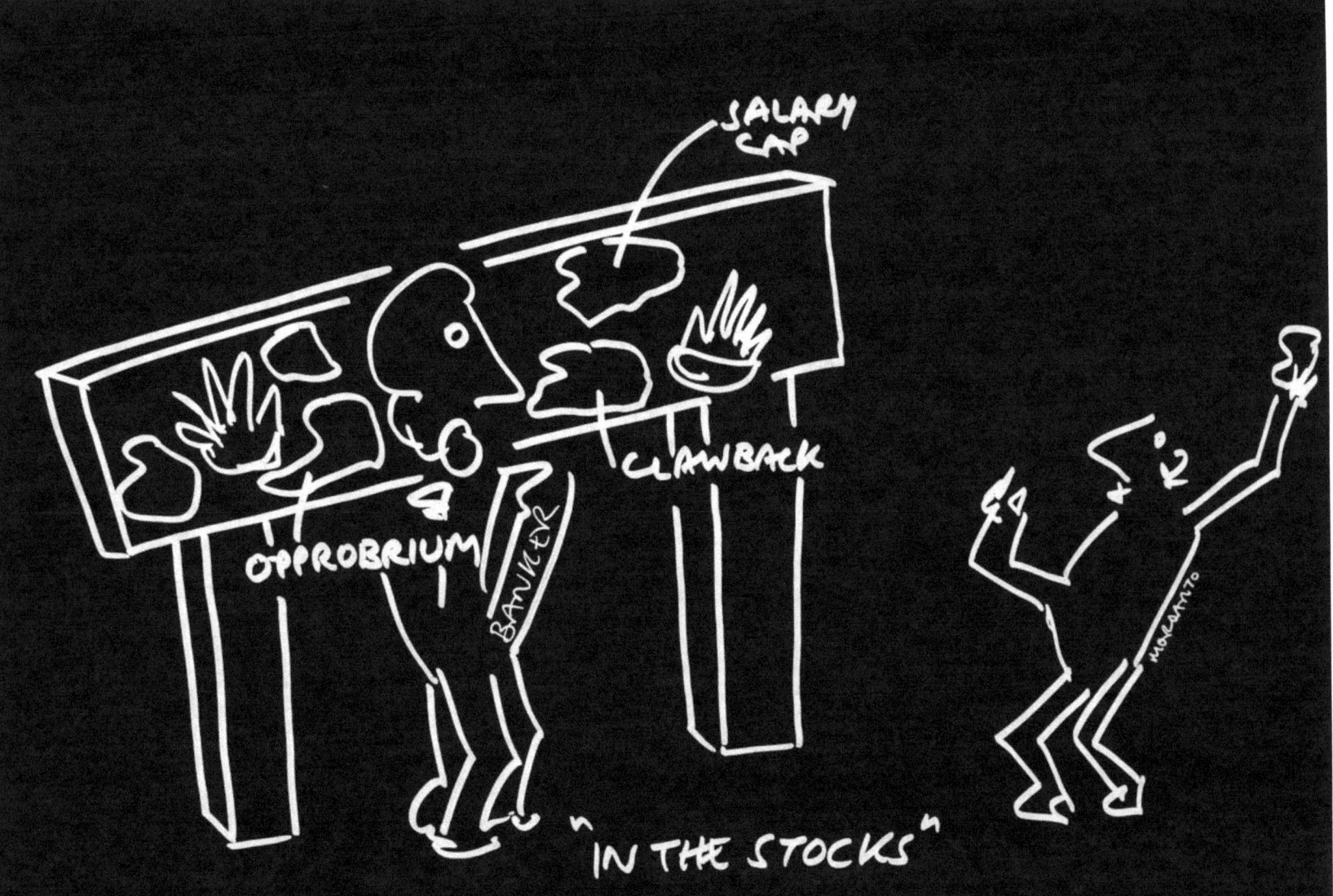

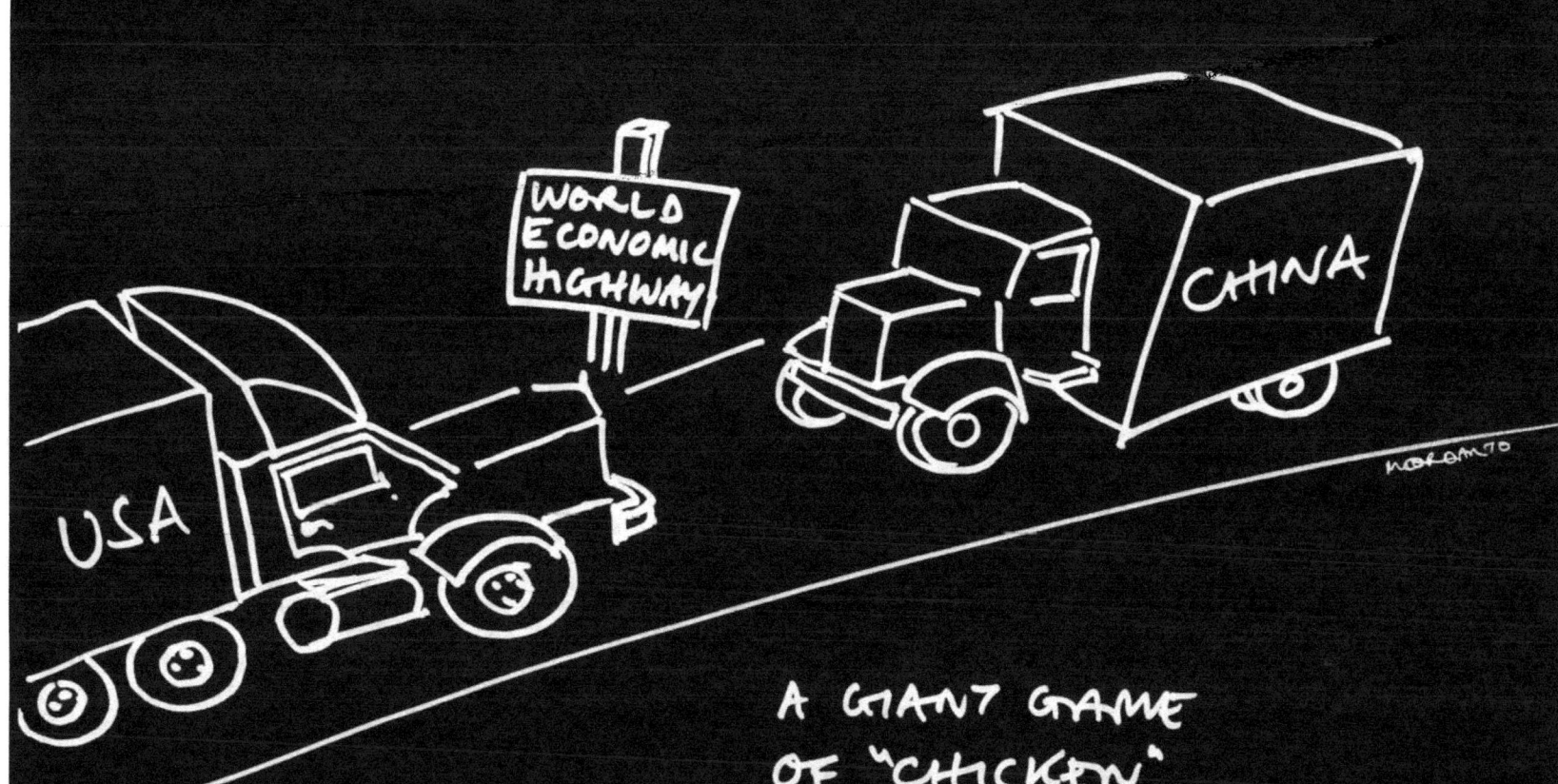

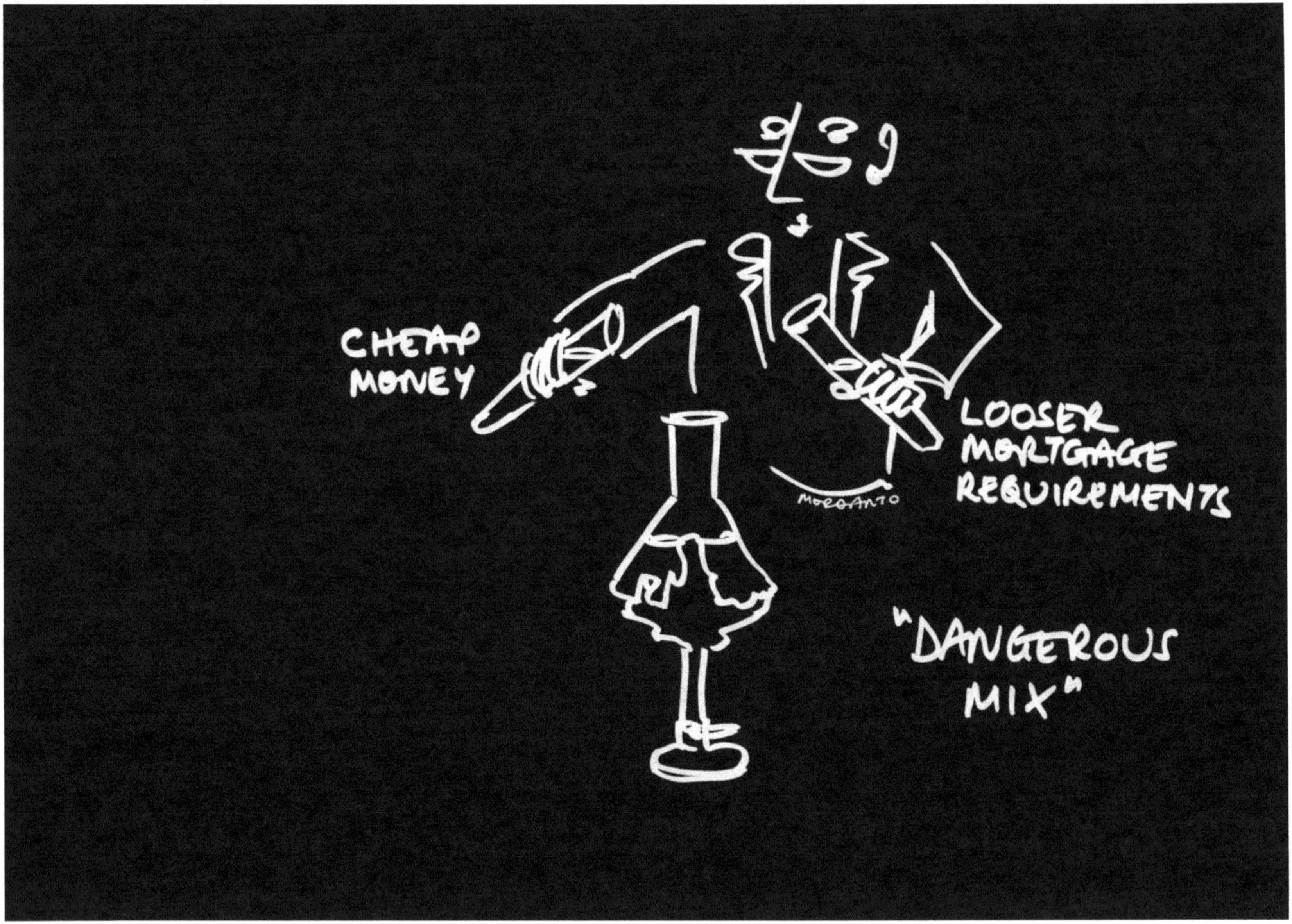
CHEAP MONEY
LOOSER MORTGAGE REQUIREMENTS
MORGANTO
"DANGEROUS MIX"

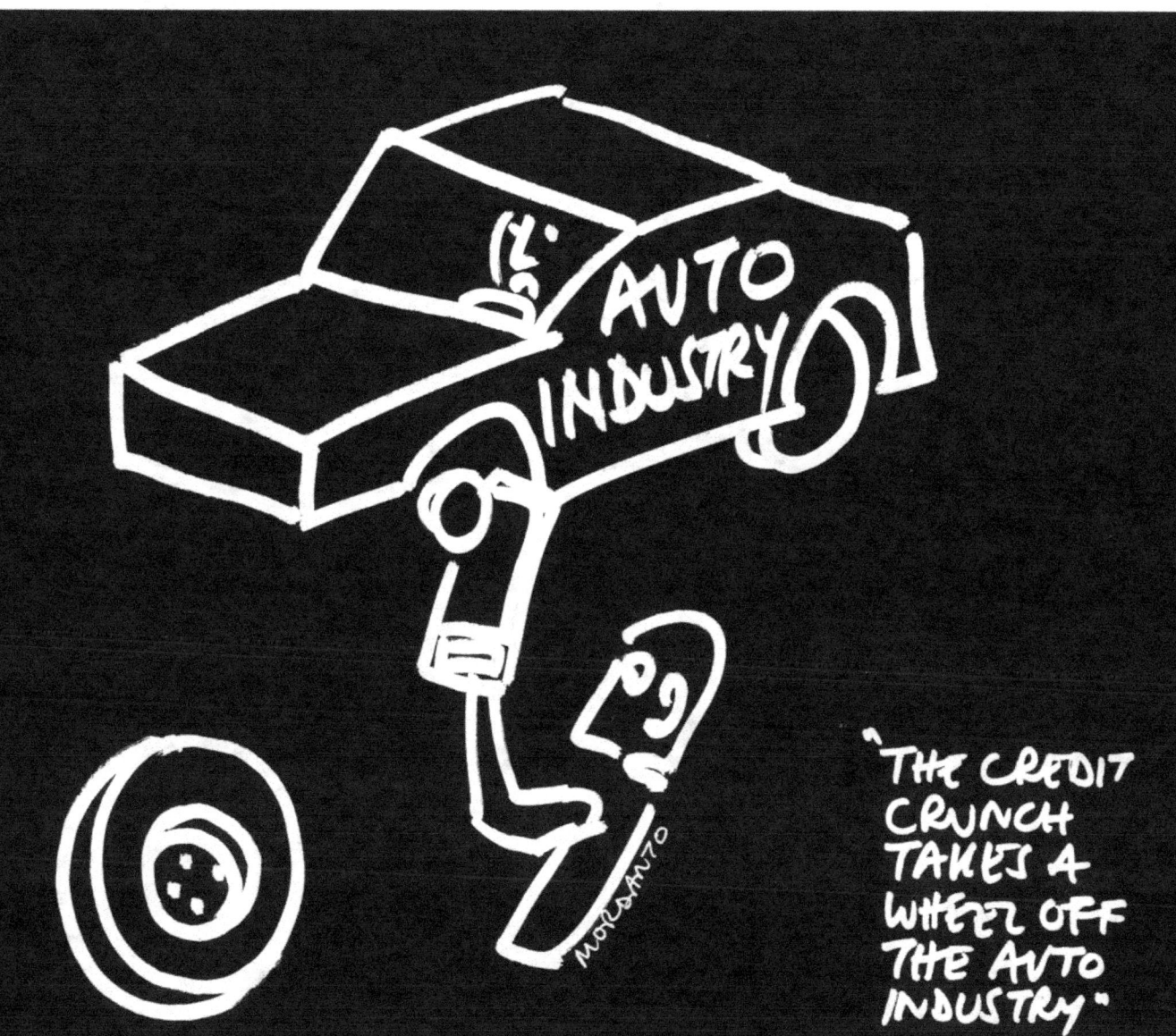

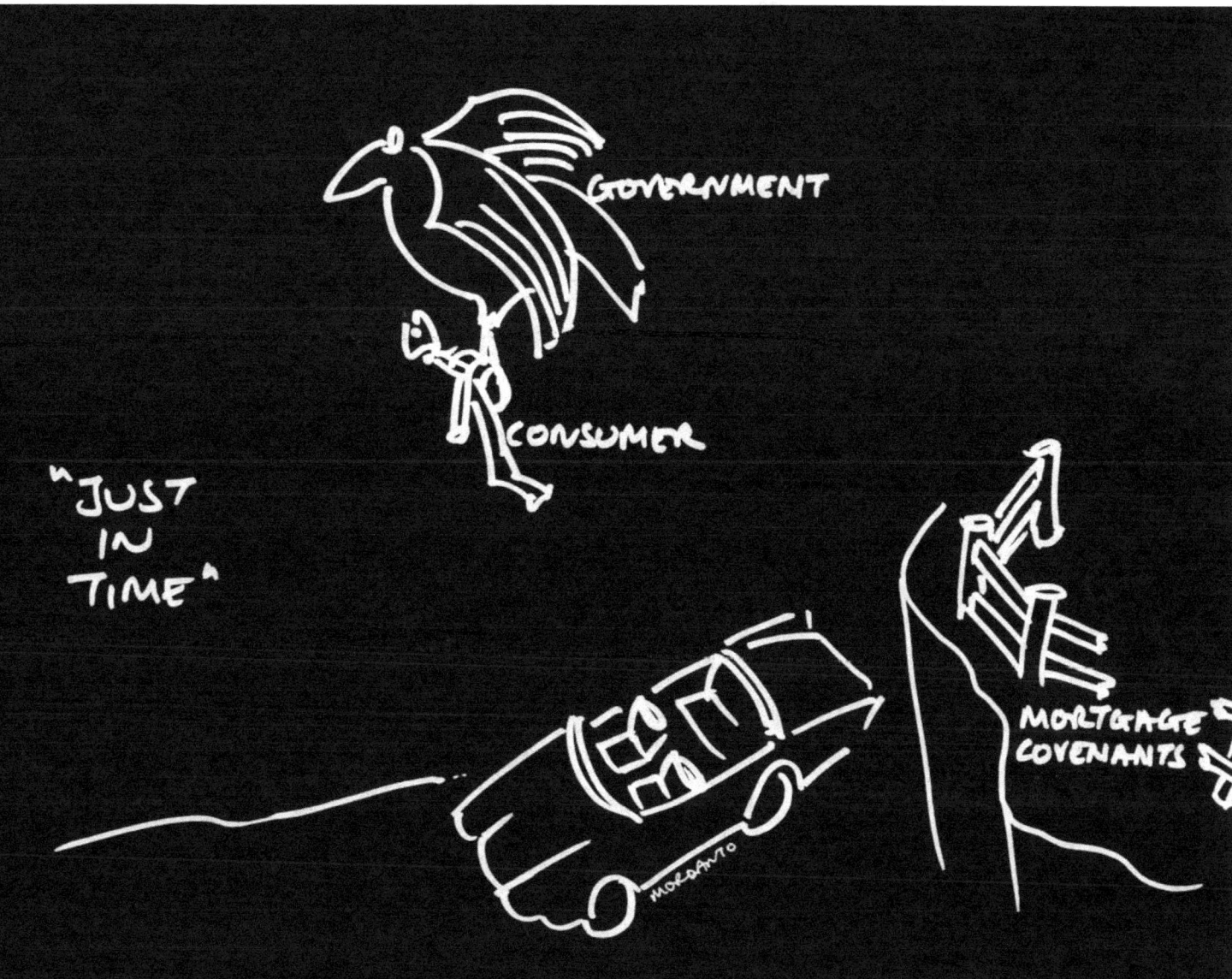

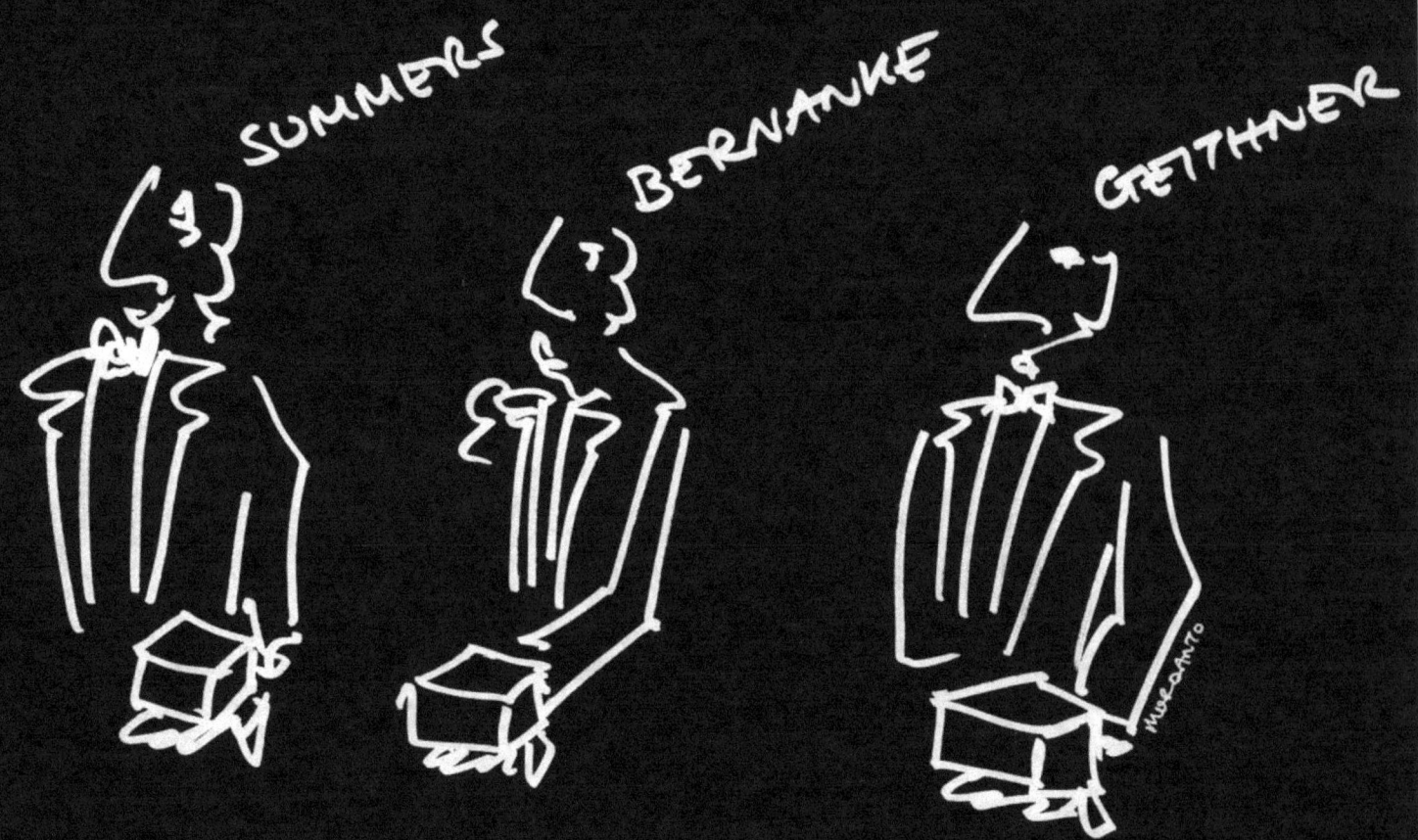

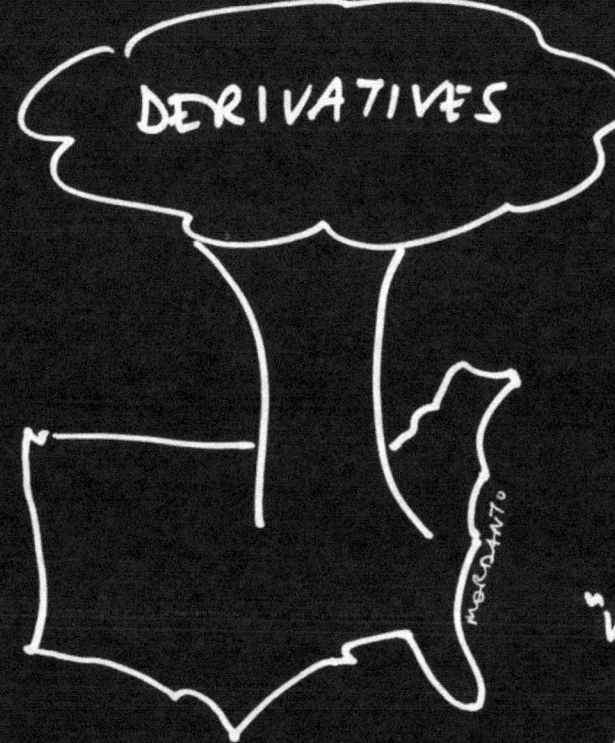

"EXPENSIVE PACEMAKER"

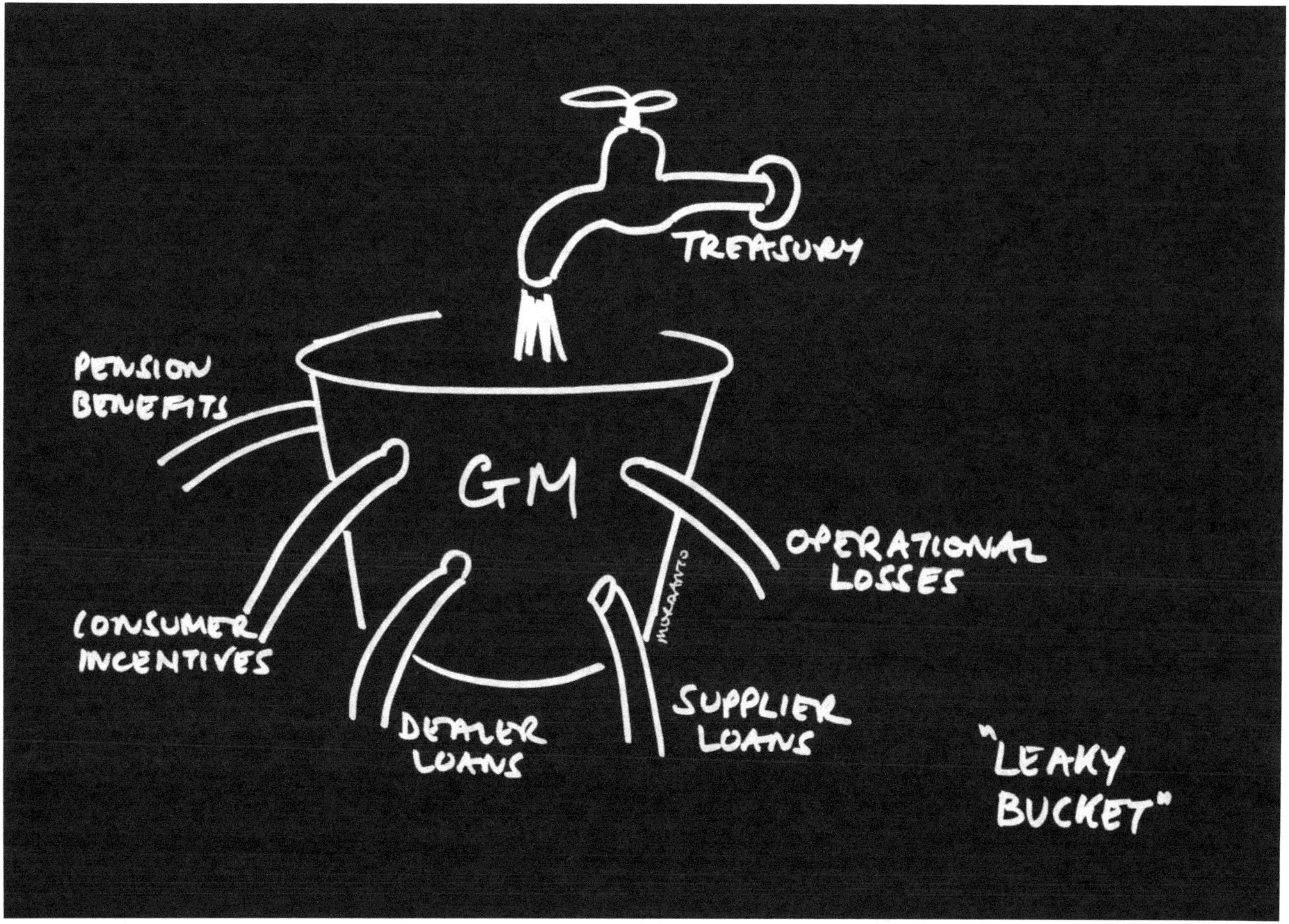

TREASURY
PENSION BENEFITS
GM
OPERATIONAL LOSSES
CONSUMER INCENTIVES
DEALER LOANS
SUPPLIER LOANS
"LEAKY BUCKET"

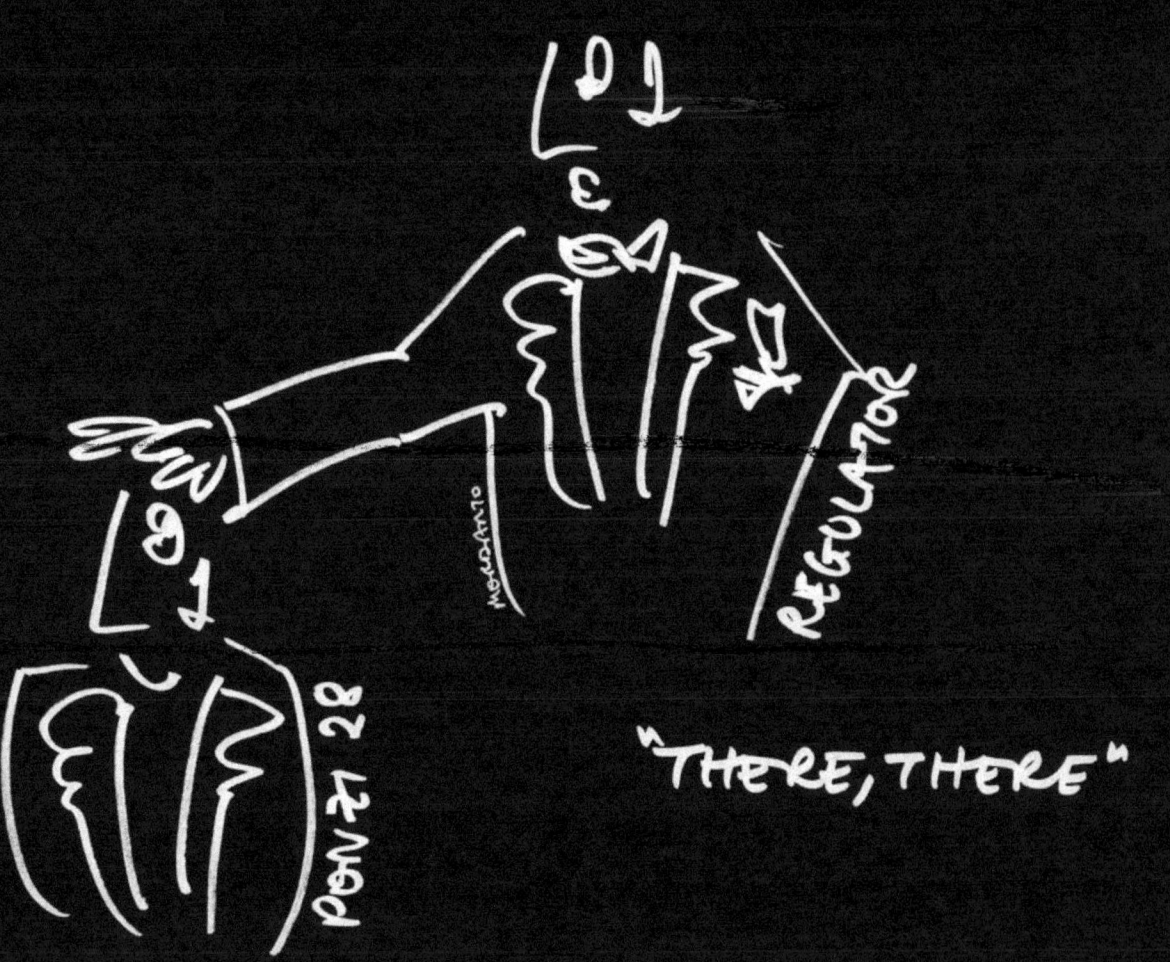

www.ingramcontent.com/pod-product-compliance
Lightning Source LLC
Chambersburg PA
CBHW081507170526
45166CB00008B/2575

9 781467 963176